Praise for *Banker to the Poor*

"By giving poor people the power to help themselves, Dr. Yunus has offered them something far more valuable than a plate of food—security in its most fundamental form."

—President Jimmy Carter

"[Yunus's] ideas have already had a great impact on the Third World, and . . . hearing his appeal for a 'poverty-free world' from the source itself can be as stirring as that all-American myth of bootstrap success." —*The Washington Post*

"I only wish every nation shared Dr. Yunus's and the Grameen Bank's appreciation of the vital role that women play in the economic, social, and political life of our societies."

—Hillary Rodham Clinton

"The [Grameen Bank] has become a mecca for development economists and is being copied around the world."

—*The Economist*

"Muhammad Yunus is a practical visionary who has improved the lives of millions of people in his native Bangladesh and elsewhere in the world. *Banker to the Poor* [is] well-reasoned yet passionate."

—*Los Angeles Times*

"Microcredit has proved its worth among the poorest."

—*The International Herald Tribune*

"Yunus shows that micro-lending can be much more effective than unwieldy and expensive aid programs." —*Publishers Weekly*

"*Banker to the Poor* offers a challenging look at the way we reinforce poverty—offering welfare instead of encouraging self-sufficiency, only offering loans to candidates with a 'safe' risk factor (what Yunus calls a 'financial apartheid'), believing that the poor lack skills and can only be worthwhile contributors to the economy after extensive training. Yunus lays out a convincing argument for the need to nourish and better understand the 'people's economy'. . . . A hopeful and inspiring read, even for those who, like me, have little prior knowledge or understanding of financing and credit loans."   —*Vision Magazine*

"An inspiring memoir of the birth of microcredit, written in a conversational tone that makes it both moving and enjoyable to read."
—*Election2004.com*

"Fascinating."   —*Hungry Mind Review*

"A fascinating and compelling account by someone who decided to make a difference, and did."   —*Choice*

Muhammad Yunus

BANKER

TO

THE

POOR

Micro-Lending

and the Battle

Against World Poverty

 PublicAffairs
NEW YORK

WITH ALAN JOLIS

Acknowledgments

For their assistance in the preparation of this edition of the book, I would like to acknowledge Alex Counts, President of Grameen Foundation USA, Kate Darnton of PublicAffairs, and for his generous support, George Stephanopoulos.

Book design by Jenny Dossin.

Library of Congress Cataloging-in-Publication Data

Yunus, Muhammad, 1940-

   Banker to the poor : micro-lending and the battle against world poverty / Muhammad Yunus with Alan Jolis.

   p. cm.

Originally published: © JC Lattès 1997.

Includes index.

ISBN-13 978-1-58648-198-8 ISBN-10 1-58648-198-3

1. Grameen Bank—History. 2. Yunus, Muhammad. 1940- . 3. Economists—Bangladesh—

Biography. 4. Rural poor—Bangladesh—History. 5. Microfinance—Bangla-desh—History. I. Jolis, Alan. II. Title.

HG3290.6.A6Y86 1999

332.'1095492—dc21   99-13535

                                                       CIP

30   29   28   27   26   25

CONTENTS

In the year 1974 Bangladesh fell into the grip of famine.

The university where I taught and served as head of the Economics Department was located in the southeastern extremity of the country, and at first we did not pay much attention to the newspaper stories of death and starvation in the remote villages of the north. But then skeleton-like people began showing up in the railway stations and bus stations of the capital, Dhaka. Soon this trickle became a flood. Hungry people were everywhere. Often they sat so still that one could not be sure whether they were alive or dead. They all looked alike: men, women, children. Old people looked like children, and children looked like old people.

The government opened gruel kitchens. But every new gruel kitchen ran out of rice. Newspaper reporters tried to warn the nation of the extent of the famine. Research institutions collected statistics on the sources and causes of the sudden migration to the cities. Religious organizations mobilized groups to pick up the dead bodies from the streets and bury them with the proper rites. But soon the simple act of collecting the dead became a larger task then these groups were equipped to handle.

The starving people did not chant any slogans. They did not demand anything from us well-fed city folk. They simply lay down very quietly on our doorsteps and waited to die.

There are many ways for people to die, but somehow dying of starvation is the most unacceptable of all. It happens in slow motion. Second by second, the distance between life and death becomes smaller and smaller, until the two are in such close proximity that one can hardly tell the difference. Like sleep, death by starvation happens so quietly, so inexorably, one does not even sense it happening. And all for lack of a handful of rice at each meal. In this world of plenty, a tiny baby, who does not yet understand the mystery of the world, is allowed to cry and cry and finally fall asleep without the milk she needs to survive. The next day she may not have the strength to continue living.

I used to feel a thrill at teaching my students the elegant economic theories that could supposedly cure societal problems of all types. But in 1974, I started to dread my own lectures. What good were all my complex theories when people were dying of starvation on the sidewalks and porches across from my lecture hall? My lessons were like the American movies where the good guys always win. But when I emerged from the comfort of the classroom, I was faced with the reality of the city streets. Here good guys were mercilessly beaten and trampled. Daily life was getting worse, and the poor were growing even poorer.

Nothing in the economic theories I taught reflected the life around me. How could I go on telling my students make-believe stories in the name of economics? I wanted to become a fugitive from academic life. I needed to run away from these theories and from my textbooks and discover the real-life economics of a poor person's existence.

I was lucky that the village of Jobra happened to be close to the campus. In 1958, Field Marshall Ayub Khan, then president of Pakistan, had taken power in a military coup. Because of his fear of rebellious students, he decreed that all new universities be situated away from urban centers. His fear of political agitation meant that the new Chittagong University, where I was teaching, was built in a hilly section of the rural Chittagong District, next to Jobra village.

The proximity of Jobra made it a perfect choice for my new course of study. I decided I would become a student all over again, and the people of Jobra would be my professors. I vowed to learn as much as possible about the village. Traditional universities had created an enormous distance between their students and the reality of everyday life in Bangladesh. Instead of traditional book learning, I wanted to teach my university students how to understand the life of one single poor person. When you hold the world in your palm and inspect it only from a bird's eye view, you tend to become arrogant—you do not realize that things get blurred when seen from an enormous distance. I opted instead for "the worm's eye view." I hoped that if I studied poverty at close range, I would understand it more keenly.

My repeated trips to the villages around the Chittagong University campus led me to discoveries that were essential to establishing the Grameen Bank. The poor taught me an entirely new economics. I learned about the problems that they face from their own perspective. I tried a great number of things. Some worked. Others did not. One that worked well was to offer people tiny loans for self-employment. These loans provided a starting point for cottage industries and other income-generating activities that used the skills the borrowers already had.

I never imagined that my micro-lending program would be the basis for a nationwide "bank for the poor" serving 2.5 million people or that it would be adapted in more than one hundred countries spanning five continents. I was only trying to relieve my guilt and satisfy my desire to be useful to a few starving human beings. But it did not stop with a few people. Those who borrowed and survived would not let it. And after a while, neither would I.

CHAPTER

ONE

Number 20

Boxirhat Road,

Chittagong

Chittagong, the largest port in Bangladesh, is a commercial city of 3 million people. I grew up on Boxirhat Road in the heart of Chittagong's old business district. A busy one-way lane, just wide enough for one truck to pass, Boxirhat Road connected the river port of Chaktai to the central produce market.

Our section of the road lay in Sonapotti, the jeweler's section. We lived at Number 20, a small two-story house with my father's jewelry shop workshop tucked beneath us on the ground floor. When I was a boy, my world was full of the noise and gasoline fumes of the street. Trucks and carts were forever blocking our road, and all day long I would hear drivers arguing, yelling, and blaring their horns. It was a sort of permanent carnival atmosphere. When toward midnight the calls of passing street vendors, jugglers, and beggars finally subsided, the sounds of hammering, filing, and polishing in my father's workshop took over.

On the upper floor, we occupied just a kitchen and four rooms: Mother's Room, Radio Room, Big Room, and a dining room where a mat was spread out three times a day for our family meals. Our playground was the flat roof above. And when we got bored, we often idled away our time watching the customers downstairs or the gold artisans at work in the back room, or we would just look out at the endlessly changing street scenes.

Number 20 Boxirhat Road was my father's second business location in Chittagong. He had abandoned the first when it was damaged
by a Japanese bomb. In 1943, the Japanese had invaded neighboring
Burma and were threatening all of India. In Chittagong, however,
the air battles were never intensive. Instead of bombs, the Japanese
planes dropped mostly leaflets, which we loved to watch from the
rooftop as they floated like butterflies down over the city. But when a
wall of our second house was destroyed by a Japanese bomb, my father promptly shifted us to the safety of his family village, Bathua,
where I had been born at the beginning of the war.

Bathua is some seven miles from Chittagong. My grandfather
owned land there, and a major part of his income came from
farming, but he gravitated toward the jewelry trade. Dula Mia, his
eldest son (and my father), also entered the jewelry business and
soon became the foremost local manufacturer and seller of jewelry ornaments for Muslim customers. Father was a soft-hearted
person. He rarely punished us, but he was strict about our need to
study. He had three iron safes, each four feet high, built into the
wall at the back of his store behind the counter. When the store
was open for business, he left the safes open. With the insides of
their heavy doors covered in mirrors and display racks, they appeared to be not safes at all, but part of the decor. Before the fifth
prayer of the day, at closing time, father would push the drawers
of the safes shut. To this day I would recognize the squeal of those
ungreased hinges and the sound of six locks on each safe clicking
shut. These sounds gave my older brother Salam and me just
enough time to stop whatever we were doing and to leap back to
our books. As long as Father saw us seated with our reading, he
would be happy and say, "Good children, good boys." Then he
would make his way to the mosque for prayer.

My father has been a devout Muslim all his life. He made three
pilgrimages to Mecca and he usually dressed all in white, with
white slippers, white pajama pants, a white tunic, and a white

prayer cap. His square tortoiseshell glasses and his gray beard gave him the look of an intellectual, but he was never a bookworm. With his large family and his successful business, he had little time or inclination to look over our lessons. Instead, he divided his life between his work, his prayers, and his family.

In contrast to Father, my mother, Sofia Khatun, was a strong and decisive woman. She was the disciplinarian of the family, and once she bit her lower lip, we knew that it was useless to try to change her mind. She wanted us all to be as methodical as she was. She was probably the strongest influence on me. Full of compassion and kindness, Mother always put money away for any poor relatives who visited us from distant villages. It was she, by her concern for the poor and the disadvantaged, who helped me discover my interest in economics and social reform.

Mother came from a family of minor merchants and traders who bought and sold goods from Burma. Her father owned land and leased most of it out. He spent most of his time reading, writing chronicles, and eating good food. It was this last trait that most endeared him to his grandchildren. In these early years, I remember my mother often wearing a bright-colored sari with a gold band around the hem. Her dark black hair was always combed into a thick bun and parted in the front to the right. I loved her very much and was certainly the one who most often pulled at her sari and demanded attention. Above all, I remember her stories and songs, such as the tragic tale of the Karbala. Every year, during Moharram—the Muslim commemoration of the Karbala—I remember asking my mother, "Mother, why is the sky red on this side of the house and blue on the other side?"

"The blue for Hassan," she would answer, "and the red for Hussein."

"Who are Hassan and Hussein?"

"They were the grandsons of our prophet—peace be upon him—the gems of his two holy eyes."

And when she finished the story of their murder, she would point to the dusk and explain that the blue on one side of the house was the poison that killed Hassan and the red on the other side was the blood of the slain Hussein. To me as a child, her depiction of this tragedy was no less moving than our great Bengali epic *Bishad Shindhu* ("The Sea of Sorrow").

Mother dominated my early years. Whenever she would fry her *pitha* cakes in the kitchen, we would crowd around her, scrambling for a taste. As soon as she slipped her first *pitha* from the frying pan and blew on it to cool it, I would snatch it from her, for I had the family distinction of being her chief taster.

Mother also worked on some of the jewelry sold in our shop. She often gave a final touch to earrings and necklaces by adding a bit of velvet ribbon or woolen pompoms or by attaching braided colored strands. I would watch as her long thin hands worked away at the beautiful ornaments. It was the money she earned on these projects that she gave away to the neediest relatives, friends, or neighbors who came to her for help.

Mother had fourteen children, five of whom died young. My elder sister, Momtaz, eight years older than me, married when she was still a teenager. We often visited in her new home at the edge of town, where she served us lavish meals. Salam, three years older than I, was my closest companion. We played war, mimicking the sounds of Japanese machine guns. And when the wind was right, we built colorful kites from diamond-shaped pieces of paper and bamboo sticks. Once Father bought a few defused Japanese shells in the market and we helped Mother transform them into plant pots for the roof by standing them on their fins, wide end up.

Salam and I, along with all the boys of our working-class neighborhood, attended the nearby Lamar Bazar Free Primary School. Bengali schools inculcate good values in the children. They aim not only for scholastic achievement but also teach civic pride; the importance of spiritual beliefs; admiration for art, music, and poetry; and respect for authority and discipline. In the Lamar Bazar Free

Primary School, each classroom had about forty students. Primary and secondary schools were not coeducational. All of us there, even the teachers, spoke in Chittagonian dialect. Good students could win scholarships and were often asked to compete in nationwide exams. But most of my fellow schoolmates soon dropped out.

Salam and I devoured any books and magazines we could get our hands on. Detective thrillers were my favorite. I even wrote one, a complete whodunit, at the age of twelve. But it was not easy to keep our thirst for reading satiated. To meet our needs, Salam and I learned to improvise, buy, borrow, and steal. For instance, our favorite children's magazine, *Shuktara*, held a yearly contest. The winners of the contest received a free subscription and had their names printed in the magazine. I picked one of the winners at random and wrote to the editor:

> Dear Sir,
>   I am so-and-so, a contest winner, and we have moved. From now on, please mail my free subscription to Boxirhat Road Number —.

I did not give our exact address, but a neighbor's, so that my father would not see the magazine. Every month, Salam and I kept our eyes peeled for our free copy. It worked like a dream.

We also spent part of every day in the waiting room of our family physician, Dr. Banik—just around the corner—reading the various newspapers he subscribed to. This freelance reading stood me in good stead over the years. Through primary and secondary school, I was often at the top of my class.

■

In 1947, when I was seven, the "Pakistan movement" reached its peak. Areas of India with Muslim majorities were fighting to become an independent Muslim state. With its Muslim majority, we knew that Chittagong would be included in Pakistan, but we were not sure what other areas of Muslim Bengal would be included or what exact boundaries would be drawn.

Friends and relatives argued endlessly at 20 Boxhirat Road about the future of an independent Pakistan. We all realized it would be a most curious country, with its western and eastern halves separated by more than one thousand miles of Indian territory. My father, a devout Muslim, had many Hindu friends and colleagues who came to our house, but even as a child I sensed the mistrust between the two religious groups. On the radio I heard about the violent riots between Hindus and Muslims. Mercifully, there was little of this in Chittagong.

My parents were deeply committed to partition from the rest of India. When my little brother Ibrahim started to speak, he called white sugar, which he liked, "Jinnah sugar," and brown sugar, which he did not like, "Gandhi sugar." Mohammed Ali Jinnah was the leader of the Pakistan partition movement, and Gandhi, of course, wanted to keep India whole. At night Mother mixed Jinnah, Gandhi, and Lord Louis Mountbatten into our bedtime stories. And my brother Salam, though only ten, envied the bigger boys in the neighborhood who carried the green flag with the white crescent and star and chanted, "Pakistan Zindabad" ("Long live Pakistan") in the street.

At midnight on August 14, 1947, the Indian subcontinent, which had been under British rule for nearly two centuries, was granted its independence. I recall it all as if it were yesterday. The whole city was decorated with flags and green and white festoons. Outside I could hear the blaring of political speeches, interrupted every so often by the chant, "Pakistan Zindabad." By midnight our street was crammed with people. We set off fireworks from the rooftop. All around I could see the silhouettes of our neighbors staring up as the exploding fireworks filled the night sky. The whole town throbbed with excitement.

As midnight approached, Father led us down into Boxhirat Road. Though he was not a political activist, he had joined the Muslim League National Guard as a gesture of solidarity, and that night he proudly wore his guard uniform, complete with the characteristic "Jinnah cap." Even my younger siblings, two-year-old Ibrahim and little baby Tunu, were with us. Exactly at midnight, the electricity was switched off, and the entire city was plunged into darkness. The next moment, when the lights came back on, we were a new country. The roaring slogan resounded again and again, from every part of Chittagong—"Pakistan Zindabad! Pakistan Zindabad!" I was seven and this was the first shot of national pride I had felt in my veins. It was intoxicating.

■

After Momtaz, Salam, myself, Ibrahim, and Tunu, my mother gave birth to four more boys: Ayub, Azam, Jahangir, and Moinu. But when I was nine, my beloved mother started becoming irritable for no apparent reason. Her behavior was increasingly abnormal. In her calmer periods she would talk disjointed nonsense to herself. For hours on end she would sit in prayer, read the same page of a book, or recite a poem over and over without stopping. In her more disturbed periods, she would insult people in a loud voice and use vulgar language. Sometimes she would hurl abuse at a neighbor, a friend, or a family member, but other times she would rant away at politicians or even long-dead figures. Her mind would turn against imaginary enemies, and then, without much warning, she would become violent. Often at night she would erupt in shouts and physical attacks, and I would help Father restrain her or try to protect my younger siblings from her blows. After such crises, she would often return to being the sweet, soft mother we remembered, giving us as much love as she could, taking care of the younger ones. But we knew that the recovery was temporary. As her condition worsened, she gradually lost track of our schooling and studies.

My father tried everything to cure her. He paid for the most advanced medical tests available in the country. As Mother's own mother and two sisters had suffered from mental illness, we assumed her condition must be congenital, but no doctor was ever able to diagnose it. In despair, my father turned to unorthodox remedies such as opium treatments, incantations, and even hypnosis. Mother never cooperated with any of these treatments, however, and none of them were successful.

At least we children found the treatments interesting. After watching a renowned psychologist apply posthypnotic suggestions to Mother, we performed our own hypnotic experiments on one another. We also learned to treat her condition with a certain humor. "What is the weather forecast?" we would ask one another when we tried to predict Mother's mood for the next few hours. To avoid provoking a fresh bout of abuse, we gave code names to various persons in the household: Number 2, Number 4, and so on. My brother Ibrahim even wrote a hilarious skit, in which he called our home a radio station, with Mother always "on air," broadcasting her sermons in various languages and moods with "active accompaniments."

The one who shone brightly through this whole sad period was my father. He adapted himself to the situation with grace and fortitude, caring for Mother in every possible way and in all circumstances for the thirty-three years that her disease lasted. He tried to behave as if nothing had changed and she was the same Sofia Khatun he had married in 1930, when he was only twenty-two. He was loyal and good to her all the fifty-two years of their marriage until her death in 1982.

■

Although Father did not mind spending money on our education and travels, he kept an extremely simple household and gave us little pocket money. In high school, the monthly stipend I received by winning the Competitive Scholarship Examination in the Chittagong District provided me with some pocket money, but not enough. I acquired the balance from Father's drawer of loose change. Father never detected this. In addition to our interest in books and magazines, Salam and I had developed a weakness for movies and eating out. Our palates were not sophisticated. My favorite dish was "potato chop," a roast potato filled with fried onion and sprinkled with vinegar. Salam and I ate these with a cup of jasmine tea at the simple tea stall around the corner from our house. Father was not privy to these outings.

The first camera that Salam and I bought was a simple box camera. It accompanied us everywhere. We researched and planned our subjects like experts: portraits, street scenes, houses, still lifes. Our accomplice in photography was the owner of a neighboring photo shop named the Mystery House Studio. He allowed us to use his darkroom to develop and print our black-and-white film. We tried special effects and even retouched our photos in color.

I became interested in painting and drawing and apprenticed with a commercial artist, whom I called *Ustad,* or "Guru." At home I arranged my easel, canvas, and pastels so that I could hide them from Father at a moment's notice. As a devout Muslim, Father did not believe in reproducing the human figure. Some art-loving uncles and aunts in the family became my coconspirators, helping and encouraging me.

As a by-product of these hobbies, Salam and I developed an interest in graphics and design. We also started a stamp collection and convinced a neighboring shopkeeper to display our stamp box in the front of his shop. With two uncles we frequented theaters to see Hindi and Hollywood films and to sing the romantic folk songs that were popular at that time.

Chittagong Collegiate School was much more cosmopolitan than my primary school had been. My classmates were mostly sons of government officials on transfer from various districts and the school offered one of the best educations in the country. But its particular attraction for me was the Boy Scout program. The scout den became my hangout. Along with boys from other schools, I engaged in drills, games, artistic pursuits, discussions, hikes in the countryside, variety shows, and rallies. During "earnings week" we would raise money by hawking goods, polishing boots, and working as tea stall boys. Aside from the fun, scouting taught me to be compassionate, to develop an inner spirituality, and to cherish my fellow human beings.

I particularly recall a train trip across India to the First Pakistan National Boy Scout Jamboree in 1953. Along the way, we stopped and visited various historical sites. Most of the time, we sang and played, but standing in front of the Taj Mahal in Agra, I caught our assistant headmaster, Quazi Sirajul Huq, weeping silently. His tears were not for the monument or for the famous lovers who are buried there or for the poetry etched on the white marble walls. Quazi Sahib said he cried for our destiny and for the burden of history that we were carrying. Though I was only thirteen, I was struck by his passionate explanation. With his encouragement, scouting began to infiltrate all my other activities. I had always been a natural leader, but Quazi Sahib's moral influence taught me to think high and to channel my passions.

In 1973, in the chaotic months following the Bangladesh War of Liberation, I visited Quazi Sahib with my father and brother Ibrahim. We drank tea and discussed the political turmoil around us. A month later, Quazi Sahib, then a frail old man, was brutally murdered in his sleep by his servant, who robbed him of a small sum of money. The police never caught the murderer. I was devastated. In retrospect, I came to understand his tears at the Taj Mahal as prophetic of both his own suffering and the suffering in store for the Bengali people.

CHAPTER

TWO

A Bengali in America

I have always thought of myself as a teacher. Even as a child, I loved instructing my younger brothers and insisted that they get only top grades in school. Immediately out of college, at the age of twenty-one, I was offered a post as a teacher of economics in my old college at Chittagong. The college, established by the British in 1836, was one of the most highly respected in the subcontinent. I taught there from 1961 until 1965.

During this time I also tried my hand at private business. I had noticed that packaging materials tended to be imported from western Pakistan and that we in the eastern half of the country had no facilities to produce boxes or wrapping material. I persuaded my father to allow me to set up a packaging and printing plant. I prepared a project proposal and applied for a loan from the government-owned Industrial Bank. At that time very few Bengali entrepreneurs wanted to set up industrial units. Our loan was immediately approved. I quickly set up a packaging and printing plant, which employed 100 workers. Over time it turned out to be a successful project making a healthy yearly profit.

My father, who was the chairman of the board, was extremely reluctant to have the company borrow from a bank. The whole notion of commercial credit made him so nervous that he made me pay the loan back early. We were probably one of the only start-up businesses in Bangladesh at that time that repaid a loan before it was due. The bank immediately offered us an additional 10 million taka loan to set up a paper plant, but my father would not hear of it.

The center of the packaging industry was in Lahore, West Pakistan. But as a nationalist Bengali, I knew we could manufacture our products cheaper in East Pakistan. Our products included cigarette packages, boxes, cartons, cosmetics boxes, cards, calendars, and books. Earning money had never been a worry of mine, but the success of the packaging factory convinced my family and me that I could excel in business if I wanted to.

Despite my success, I still wanted to study and teach. So when I was offered a Fulbright scholarship in 1965, I jumped at the chance to get a Ph.D. in the United States. This would be my third trip abroad. As a Boy Scout I had gone to the World Jamboree in Niagara Falls, Canada, in 1955 and to Japan and the Philippines in 1959. But this time I was on my own and I was in for some surprises. At first the University of Colorado campus in Boulder was quite a shock. In Bangladesh, students would never dare to call professors by their first names. If one spoke to "sir," it was only after being invited by "sir" to speak, and then one spoke in enormously respectful terms. But in Boulder, teachers seemed to consider themselves friends of the students. I often saw faculty and students sprawled out on the lawn barefoot, sharing food, joking, and chatting. Such familiarity was totally unthinkable in Bangladesh. And as for the young coeds in Colorado, well, I was so shy and embarrassed I did not know where to look. At Chittagong College, female students were distinctly in the minority. Of a student body of 800, no more than 150 were women. Women were also segregated. They were usually confined to the Women's Common Room, which was off-limits to male students. Their participation in the student politics and in other activities was limited. When we staged plays, for example, women were not allowed to participate, so men wearing women's dress and makeup would take on female roles.

My female students at Chittagong University were extremely shy. When it was time for class, they would huddle in a group just outside the Teachers' Common Room and then follow me to class, clutching their books and looking down at their feet so as to avoid the stares of the boys. Inside the classroom they sat apart from the boys, and I learned to avoid asking them questions that could possibly embarrass them in front of their classmates. I never talked to them outside the classroom.

In fact, I myself was so shy about women that I tried to ignore them entirely. Imagine my dismay when I arrived in the United States in the summer of 1965! The campus was alive with rock music. Girls would sit on the lawn with their shoes off, sunning themselves and laughing. I was so nervous, I tried to not even look at them. But I still loved to sit in the Student Center, watching the students come and go, chatting, flirting, eating, wearing their crazy clothes. The youth of the United States looked so strong and healthy and full of vitality. It was an age of drug experimentation. Alcohol was rife. But my shy personality led me away from the raucous parties. I preferred to study in my room or watch TV.

Television had appeared in Dhaka only in 1964, and before arriving in the United States I was quite unfamiliar with it. At Boulder, I soon became addicted. My favorite show was *60 Minutes*, but I also watched every silly sitcom there was: *I Love Lucy, Gilligan's Island, Hogan's Heroes*. I found I could talk and think more clearly when the TV was on. That is still true today.

This was also the height of the Vietnam War, and along with other foreign students I joined antiwar rallies and protest marches. Though I voiced my opposition to the Vietnam War, I tried to keep an open mind and not merely to spout what was fashionable or veer into groupthink. My leftist Bengali friends could not understand my positive opinions about the United States.

Back in Dhaka, there was a lot of anti-American sentiment. Students on every campus called the United States dirty capitalists, shouting, "Yankee, Go Home!"

Quickly, I learned to enjoy the personal freedom of the United States. I started having fun. My studies were going well and I even found time to learn square dancing. I got quite used to seeing people drinking wine, beer, and strong alcohol. Little everyday incidents made a great impression on me. I will never forget the first time I entered a restaurant in Boulder to have the waitress say, "Hi, my name is Cheryl," and offer me a big smile and a glass of water with lots of ice in it. No one in my country or in South Asia would ever treat a stranger so openly and forthrightly.

As for American food, I missed my mother's spicy cooking. As much as I liked French fries, hamburgers, potato chips, and ketchup, I was heartily bored with American food, and I would have given anything in the world to eat rice and dal, or Bengali sweetmeats.

My summer in Boulder, surrounded by students from many different countries and a beautiful sunlit campus, passed all too quickly. In the fall, my scholarship required me to attend Vanderbilt University in Tennessee, where I had a completely different experience. Nashville was depressing and unattractive after the wide-open vistas of Colorado. Also, Vanderbilt had only recently been desegregated. Even the tiny restaurant I frequented, the Campus Grill, had been "For Whites Only" six months earlier. There were few foreign students and no Bengalis. I felt lonely and homesick. The winter was cold and my dormitory, Wesley Hall, was so smelly that we quickly renamed it "Wesley Hell." The heating pipes banged and knocked all night long. The showers had old-fashioned open stalls and I was so shy and prudish that I took to showering in a *lungi*, a full-length skirt worn by people in Bangladesh.

I was the only Fulbright scholar at Vanderbilt that year. At first, my classes bored me. My graduate program in economic development was a "light master's," superficial compared to the far more advanced work I had already done in Bangladesh. Luckily, however, I was soon placed on a Ph.D. track and fell under the wing of a famous Romanian professor by the name of Nicholas Georgescu-Roegen.

Professor Georgescu-Roegen was known as a terror on campus. He flunked many students and it was rumored that he ruined many students' academic careers. But I thought he was wonderful. He taught me simple lessons that I never forgot and precise economic models that would eventually help me build up Grameen. Through him I realized there was little need for memorizing economic formulas. Far more important was to understand the underlying concepts that drive them to work. He also taught me that things are never as complicated as they seem. It is only our arrogance that prompts us to find unnecessarily complicated answers to simple problems.

■

When I left for my Fulbright scholarship in the United States, I certainly had no intention of finding an American wife. I assumed that if and when the issue of marriage arose I would marry the way everybody around me had, by arranged marriage. I also had no experience of women and was terribly shy around them. Bengalis are quite prudish and conservative in general and even more so in the religious Chittagong District where I grew up. In my family we never discussed such intimate things openly.

So in 1967, when a beautiful girl with shoulder-length red hair and blue eyes approached me in the Vanderbilt library, I was completely unprepared. She asked me where I was from.

"Pakistan," I replied, rather nervously.

This girl was friendly, spontaneous, and particularly curious about me and my background. Her name was Vera Forostenko, and she was doing her master's work in Russian literature. Vera was born in the USSR, but she and her family came to the United States soon after the Second World War. They settled in Trenton, New Jersey. I liked her immediately.

Two years after we met, in 1969, Vera left Tennessee and moved back to New Jersey. I was already making plans to return to Bangladesh.

"I want to come live with you there," Vera said.

"You can't," I replied. I was extremely stubborn. "It's a tropical country. A different culture. Women there are not treated as they are here."

"But I will adapt," she insisted.

She kept writing to me and calling to discuss this issue. Every time I found a reason why such a move would not work, she would find a counterreason.

Finally, I changed my mind.

We were married in 1970 and moved to Murfreesboro, a town fifty miles south of Nashville, where I was teaching at Middle Tennessee State University. Life was calm and peaceful, and then, on March 25, 1971, I came back to my apartment to have lunch and turned on the radio for the latest news from Dhaka. There was a brief item stating that the Pakistani army had moved in to block all political opposition against the government of Pakistan, and that Sheikh Mujibur Rahman, leader of the independence movement, had fled.

I was changing my clothes. I stopped, rushed to the phone, and dialed Dr. Zillur Rahman Athar in Nashville. I asked him to turn on the radio and contact all the other Bengalis he knew in the area. Within an hour I was at Zillur's house. At that time there were six Bengalis from East Pakistan in greater Nashville. We began collecting news from all sources. There was no obvious consensus on the situation, but one thing was clear: The Pakistani army wanted to crush Bengalis once and for all. One of us, a supporter of the conscrvative pro-Islamic Jamaat party, kept saying, "We really don't know what has happened. Let us wait for more details."

I did not agree. "We have all the details we need," I said. "Bangladesh has declared its independence. Now we have to decide whether we consider ourselves citizens of this new country or not. Everybody has the right to choose. I declare my choice. My choice is Bangladesh. I declare my allegiance to Bangladesh. If there is any one else who would like to join me in this, he is free to do so. Those who do not join Bangladesh, I will consider Pakistani and an enemy of my country."

There was silence. Everyone was taken aback by the way I posed the question of allegiance. I suggested that we form the Bangladesh Citizens' Committee and immediately issue a press release for the Nashville print and electronic media.

We decided three things:

1. We would try to meet all the news reporters of the local TV stations and the editors of the local dailies to explain our decision and to seek support for the Bangladesh cause.

2. We would each immediately donate $1,000 to create a fund for the struggle.

3. We would give 10 percent of our monthly salary to the fund until Bangladesh became independent. If needed, we would increase the percentage.

Everybody pulled out his checkbook or borrowed from others to make the first deposit.

The next day, March 27, we made appointments with local TV stations and newspapers. I was elected secretary of the Bangladesh Citizens' Committee and spokesperson for the group. The local TV stations were thrilled. They rarely got a chance to scoop international news stories, and for them we represented a red-hot international news break with a local angle. I was a teacher in a local university, the other five were medical doctors in city hospitals, and here we were—declaring ourselves citizens of a country not yet born.

That afternoon we reassembled at Zillur's house to watch the local evening news. My interview was telecast in full. The interviewer asked, "Do you have a message for the Tennesseans?"

"Yes, I do," I replied. "Please write to your congressional representatives and senators immediately to stop military aid to Pakistan. Your arms and ammunitions are being used to kill innocent unarmed civilians of Bangladesh. Please ask your president to put pressure on Pakistan to stop genocide in Bangladesh."

I was pleased that all six of us, from differing political tendencies and socioeconomic backgrounds, had cooperated with immediate action. We now wanted to know what other Bengalis around the United States were doing. We decided to contact Mr. Enayet Karim, a Bengali official in the Pakistan embassy. He gave me some important news: There would be a demonstration against the Pakistani army's crackdown on civilians on March 29 on Capitol Hill in Washington, D.C. The biggest group of Bengalis would come from New York. He urged us to join.

Though my doctor friends could not go because of their responsibilities at the hospitals, I announced that I would leave the next day. It was decided that I would go at my own expense. I could also use the $6,000 we had already raised if there was need for it in Washington.

Where would I stay in Washington? I did not know anybody. Though I had never met Enayet Karim, he sounded like a friendly person. Why not try him? I called him again. I proposed to be his guest the next day—would he mind? He immediately told me to come right over. His hospitality surprised me. I suppose the crisis had brought all us Bengalis together.

Until midnight we monitored every single radio station on Zillur's giant shortwave radio. Between news items we ate delicious food supplied by Zillur's American wife, Joanne, and speculated on what might have happened to Sheikh Mujib.* Finally, the news came that he had been arrested at Chittagong railway station while he was fleeing from the army (he was actually arrested at his house in Dhaka). We were in tears on hearing the news. All our fantasies of Sheikh Mujib leading the nation to victory were dashed. What would the Pakistani army do with him? Bring him back to Dhaka and execute him by firing squad? Hang him? Torture him to death?

I left for Washington, D.C., in the early hours of March 28, arriving at Enayet Karim's beautiful house in the late afternoon. Mrs. Karim, who was also a native of Chittagong, welcomed me warmly. It was a busy day. The telephone never stopped ringing. Some calls were local, others from far-flung Pakistani embassies or from Bengali officials searching for policy guidelines. Thrown into the midst of this excitement, I felt like part of an already-independent Bangladesh. There was no trace of Pakistan in the minds of those in the Karim household.

While enjoying this intoxicating scene, I noticed a serious-looking man busy writing. He was Mr. S. A. Karim, the deputy permanent representative of Pakistan at the United Nations, who had arrived from New York that morning. Eventually, he wanted to read aloud what he had written. Everyone gathered around him.

---

*In 1970, Pakistan held a general election under a military government. The East Pakistan–based Awami League, under the leadership of Sheikh Mujibur Rahman ("Sheikh Mujib"), won an absolute majority in the national parliament. But the army, which was made up almost entirely of officers and soldiers from West Pakistan, refused to allow the Awami League to form a government. On March 25, 1971, they imposed a military crackdown. The people of East Pakistan responded by declaring the independence of East Pakistan and building resistance to the Pakistani army. The war of liberation for a new country, called Bangladesh, began.

He had just finished drafting an appeal to all heads of governments to put pressure on Pakistan to stop the genocide in Bangladesh.

I did not want the demonstration to be a poor show and kept trying to find out who was in charge of the next day's activities on the Hill. What preparations were being made? Was somebody preparing posters to hold up in front of the TV cameras? Nobody in Enayet Karim's house seemed to know. I thought I should take some initiative. I went to a department store and bought stacks of colored paper, paint, and brushes. Immediately I set to work making festoons, a skill I had acquired while a student at Chittagong College.

Shamsul Bari arrived. He was teaching Bangla at the University of Chicago. I had known him from a distance during our university days in Dhaka. The War of Liberation brought us close. We worked together during the entire period of the war.

By evening more people had assembled at Enayet Karim's house. Some worried about their families in Bangladesh; others wanted more information about the situation in Dhaka and what needed to be done. The night was spent analyzing the situation and deciding on the strategy for the following day: First, delivering an appeal to all embassies and heads of government, and second, organizing the demonstration on Capitol Hill. Mrs. Karim treated us as if we were her dearest friends, feeding us steaming plates of food while alternately cursing the Pakistani army and reciting Tagore poems.

The next morning, March 29, I woke up to shouting. I threw on some clothes and ran down to the anteroom, where a short, skinny person with a beard was lecturing Karim in a loud voice. The small room was packed with five or six people.

The tiny man was behaving very rudely. He kept accusing Karim and the other embassy officials of being traitors. The rest of the people in the room wore buttons printed with "BANGLADESH" in bold letters.

These visitors had driven from Harvard and other institutions in Boston to join the demonstration on Capitol Hill, and they were furious when they discovered that Bengali embassy officials had decided not to participate. The tiny man—Dr. Mohiuddin Alamgir, a fresh Ph.D. from Harvard, who became one of my closest friends—spared no harsh words in attacking Karim. I tried to defend my host, explaining that embassy officials had contacts with the high officials in the U.S. State Department who could brief them on the real situation. It was a good strategy to keep our high positions in the government so that the Pakistanis would not freely wield the power of the government against the Bengalis in East Pakistan.

Alamgir disagreed. This was only "sweet talk" by cowards who did not want to join the cause of liberation but protect their cushy lifestyle. The meeting ended in a stalemate. Only on August 4 did Bengali diplomats of the Pakistan embassy finally defect and join the Bangladesh government-in-exile.

That afternoon we all gathered at the steps of the U.S. Congress to demonstrate. Bengalis came from distant places. Washington, New York, and Detroit had the biggest contingents. I was particularly surprised to see so many Detroit factory workers who were from Sylhet District in Bangladesh.

Nobody knew quite what to do or where to go. We could not begin because we did not have official permission to demonstrate. We were still wondering how to organize ourselves when Shamsul Bari showed up with the necessary permission. I shouted at the top of my voice: "Here is our leader. Let's now line up behind him and start our demonstration."

It worked like magic. The demonstration on the steps of Capitol Hill was a grand affair. We were noticed by U.S. legislators. Congressional aides took time to be briefed on the situation and our demands. The news media were especially active; television cameras covered the rally and took on-the-spot interviews.

That evening, we all met at the residence of another official of the embassy, Mr. A. M. A. Muhith, the economic counselor. There was a heated debate over the coordination of Bengali activities in the United States and the immediate transfer of allegiance by Bengali diplomats. The shouting with which my day had begun was repeated with more intensity at this grand assembly—why were not Bengali diplomats leaving the Pakistan embassy right away? We left after dinner, knowing that we had to find a way to coordinate the activities of all Bengalis in the United States and convinced that the Bengali diplomats could no longer provide the necessary leadership. I began to doubt whether diplomats should stay on with Pakistan.

On March 30, Shamsul Bari and I were given the responsibility of visiting all the embassies, meeting the ambassadors or their representatives, explaining our cause, and requesting recognition of Bangladesh as an independent state. It was a very interesting experience. We visited many embassies in one day. Each one had its own style of receiving us, but there were many common questions: Whom do you represent? Do you have a U.S.-based organization? How can we "recognize" your country if you do not have a government? Is there any foreign government supporting you? What is the position of your diplomats in the United States? Are they supporting you? When are they going to come out in the open? What proportion of the population in "East Pakistan" wants an independent Bangladesh?

Only one question stumped us: "Do you have a government of your own?"

Bari and I decided that we had to have our own government immediately, but how does one go about establishing a government in Bangladesh while still in Washington? I had an idea: I could fly to Calcutta, find a few people to form a cabinet, and announce to the world that a Bangladesh government had been formed. In a snap, we would have both a country and a government. Bari liked the idea. We decided I would leave for Calcutta the next day.

I thought of another essential strategy—a radio station to broadcast programs for Bangladesh, so that the people inside Bangladesh knew what was going on and what they had to do. A radio transmitter, I thought, should be mounted on a vehicle. It should broadcast inside Bangladeshi territory and return to the Indian side of the border whenever chased by the Pakistani army. I had $6,000. This should cover the down payment for a transmitter.

We had some special requests for various embassies. At the Burmese embassy we asked Burma to keep its borders open to those fleeing from the Pakistani army. We would try to find funds to feed refugees from Bangladesh. At the Sri Lankan embassy we asked Sri Lanka to refuse landing rights to all Pakistani military and civilian flights between Bangladesh and Pakistan. Pakistan was known to carry army personnel, arms, and ammunition on civilian flights from Karachi to Dhaka. In the Indian embassy we were treated like highly placed diplomats. Officials there wanted to know about Bengali diplomats in the Pakistan embassy, about the whereabouts of our leaders, and whether we had established a U.S.-based organization. We asked India to open its border to refugees, provide free access to Calcutta for expatriate Bangladeshis, and relax rules surrounding Indian visas for Bengalis with Pakistani passports.

That night we had another exciting discussion about setting up a government. We slightly rearranged our earlier plan. It was decided that M. A. Hasan should leave immediately for Calcutta and Agartala to make initial contacts with the political leaders who had fled from Bangladesh. He would then send the signal for me to join him and form the new government.

That night Aga Hilali, the Pakistani ambassador, came on a courtesy visit to Enayet Karim. Several of us, who were eating dinner, were quickly pushed into an attic room with our food. We sat there for two hours without making a sound, so that the ambassador would not know that his Bengali colleague was harboring three antistate activists in his own house.

Hasan left for Calcutta and Agartala the next day as planned. From Calcutta, he sent a bitter message of disappointment in the leaders and advised me not to come. Soon after, the Mujibnagar government was formed. Bengalis in the United States and Canada concentrated on the campaign for Bangladeshi recognition, on stopping military aid to Pakistan, and on freeing Sheikh Mujib.

The Bangladesh League of America was established in New York under the leadership of Dr. Mohammad Alamgir, a physician, and in Chicago the Bangladesh Defense League was created by Dr. F. R. Khan, a Bengali-American architect who designed the Sears Tower in Chicago. Shamsul Bari became its secretary general. He published the first issue of the *Bangladesh Newsletter.* I took it over from him and published the newsletter regularly from my Nashville apartment at 500 Paragon Mills Road. My apartment became a communication center. The phone rang off the hook with calls from all over North America and the United Kingdom. All Bengalis wanted daily updates on the war.

Through the efforts of the Bengalis in Washington, the Bangladesh Information Center was also set up to do the lobbying in the House and the Senate. I took on the responsibility of running the information center for its initial period and then went on the road to organize teach-in workshops on university campuses all over the United States.

During the next nine months we drew a very clear picture of the future Bangladesh. We wanted to uphold democracy. We wanted to ensure the people's right to a free and fair election and to a life devoid of poverty. We dreamed of happiness and prosperity for all citizens and a nation that would stand with dignity among all other nations in the world.

On December 16, 1971, Bangladesh won its war of independence. The war had taken a heavy toll. Three million Bangladeshis had been killed and 10 million had left the country in search of safety in neighboring India. Millions more were the victims of rape and other atrocities committed by the Pakistani army. By the time the war was over, Bangladesh was a devastated country. The economy was shattered. Millions of people needed to be rehabilitated.

I knew that I had to return home and participate in the work of nation building. I thought I owed it to myself.

CHAPTER

THREE

Back in Chittagong

On my return to Bangladesh in 1972, I was offered a fancy title and appointed to the government's Planning Commission. My job was a bore. I had nothing to do all day but read newspapers. After repeated protests to the chief of the Planning Commission, Nurul Islam, I resigned to become head of the Economics Department at Chittagong University.

Chittagong University is located twenty miles east of the city of Chittagong on 1,900 acres of barren hills. Built in the mid-1960s from designs by a leading architect of Bangladesh, the university looks impressive. The buildings are constructed entirely of exposed red brick with open corridors and expansive rooms. But although pleasing to the eye, these modern buildings are not at all utilitarian. When I arrived, for instance, there was a huge office for the head of each department, but no office space for the rest of the teachers. One of the first things I did as head of Economics was to convert my office into a common room for my colleagues. Strangely enough, this made the staff uncomfortable. They expected the head of the department to have a big room, even if others did not have any place to sit.

It was a difficult time at the university. Teachers were refusing to grade examinations, accusing students of copying their answers from books and from each other. Many of the students were part of the Mukti Bahini (Liberation Army) and had just returned from war. They still carried their guns and threatened to harm the teachers if exam results were not announced soon.

At that time I lived with my parents in town. My father allowed me to use his car to commute to the campus every day. Along the way I drove through the village of Jobra, which stood between the highway and the campus. I noticed barren fields next to the village and asked a colleague, Professor H. I. Latifee, why they were not being cultivated for a winter crop. As he did not know, I proposed that we go talk to the villagers and find out the reason. It turned out that there was no water for irrigation.

I thought we should do something about the unused fields. It was a shame to let the land around a university campus remain barren. If a university is a repository for knowledge, then some of this knowledge should spill over to the neighboring community. A university must not be an island where academics reach out to higher and higher levels of knowledge without sharing any of their findings.

Our campus housing faced a range of hills, and from my classroom I could see a stream of boys and girls, men and cattle, walking through the campus toward the hills every morning. They carried sharp knives and at sunset they returned with loads of twigs. It occurred to me that the university should convert these hills into fertile cropland. This would bring additional income to the university, employment to the villagers, and food to the country at large.

I also grew more and more curious about the village itself. I launched a project, with my students' help, to survey Jobra's economy. We wanted to find out how many of the families in the village owned cultivable land and what crops they grew. How did people without any land make a living? What skills did the villagers have? What impediments did they see to improving their lives? How many families could grow food to feed themselves for the whole year? How many could not? Who were the poor?

Analyses of the causes of poverty focus largely on why some countries are poor rather than on why certain segments of the population live below the poverty line. Socially conscious economists stress the absence of "entitlements" of the poor. What I did not know yet about hunger, but would find out over the next twenty-two years, was that brilliant theorists of economics do not find it worthwhile to spend time discussing issues of poverty and hunger. They believe that these will be resolved when general economic prosperity increases. These economists spend all their talents detailing the processes of development and prosperity, but rarely reflect on the origin and development of poverty and hunger. As a result, poverty continues.

The 1974 famine dragged on and on, and the worse it became, the more agitated I grew. Unable to stand it any longer, I went to see the vice-chancellor of the university. A popular social commentator and novelist, Abul Fazal was considered by many to be the conscience of the nation. He greeted me politely.

"What can I do for you, Yunus?" he asked. A ceiling fan turned slowly overhead. Mosquitoes buzzed. His orderly brought tea.

"Many people are dying of starvation, yet everyone is afraid to talk about it," I responded.

Abul Fazal nodded. "What do you propose?"

"You are a respected man. I would ask you to make a statement to the press."

"Yes, but what?"

"A call to the nation and its leadership to end the famine. I am certain that all teachers on this campus will cosign their names to your letter if you take the lead. It would help mobilize national opinion."

"Yes." He sipped his tea. "Yunus," he said, "you write the statement, and I will sign it."

I smiled. "You are the writer. You will know what words to put in the statement."

"No, no, you do it, Yunus. You're passionate about this. You'll know what to say."

"But I am only an economics professor. And this document should become a rallying cry, a call to action."

The more I insisted that he was the perfect man to bring national attention to bear on the famine, the more Abul Fazal encouraged me to write the letter. He pushed his point so strongly that I had no alternative but to promise I would try. That evening I wrote out a statement. The next morning I brought the draft to the vice-chancellor and waited while he read it.

When he was finished, Abul Fazal reached for his pen and said, "Where do I sign?"

I was stunned. "But it is strongly worded. Maybe you want to change some things or suggest other ideas."

"No, no, no, it is excellent," he said. And with that he signed on the spot.

I had no choice. I signed the document as well, and I made copies of it and presented it to other faculty members. Some teachers raised objections to one word or another, but because the vice-chancellor had already signed, all of them eventually agreed to add their names to the declaration. We delivered it to the press that night, and the next day our statement was carried as a banner headline on the front pages of all the major newspapers.

Our statement started a chain reaction. Other universities and public bodies that had not spoken out against the famine took up our call. I began focusing all my efforts on farming. It was clear that Bangladesh, a territory of 35 million acres with a very dense population, needed to increase its food production. We had 21 million acres available for cultivation. In the rainy season we produced mainly rice and jute. By extending irrigation and improving water management during the dry winter season, we could increase our crops. Specialists estimated that the existing land yielded only 16 percent of our crop potential.

I decided I would experiment on the microlevel by helping the villagers of Jobra grow more food. But how would I go about it? Grow more in each crop cycle? Increase the number of crop plantings in each plot? I was not an agronomist. But I made it my business to study the low-yielding local variety of rice and more high-yielding varieties developed in the Philippines. At first the farmers were amused by my findings. But when they saw how very serious I was, they agreed to let me plant the high-yielding rice in their fields. My students and other university teachers joined the effort as volunteers. We explained to the village farmers the importance of spacing the seedlings at regular intervals and planting in a straight line to optimize crop yields. The local newspaper published photos of us, knee-deep in mud, showing local farmers how to use a string to plant rice in a straight line. Many readers were contemptuous of my hands-on approach.

Despite such skepticism, I kept trying to bring the academic world and the village together by championing a university project called the Chittagong University Rural Development Project (CURDP). Through the CURDP, I encouraged my students to go with me into the village and devise creative ways to improve day-to-day life there. By now I had almost completely abandoned classical book learning in favor of hands-on, person-to-person experience. Based on their experiences in the village, students could also choose a topic and write a research paper for course credit.

In the winter of 1975, I focused my attention on solving the problem of irrigation to raise an extra winter crop. I knew that during monsoon season almost every square meter of land was cultivated, including wasteland marshes, which produced rice and fish. Yet all these lands remained unused during winter. Why not add a winter crop? Every day I noticed an unused deep tubewell sitting idle in the middle of the uncultivated fields. It was the dry winter season, the season when the tubewell should have been irrigating the land for a new crop. But nothing was being done. The tubewell just sat there, brand new and unused.

When I asked why the tubewell was idle, I learned that the farmers were supposed to pay for the water but that they had fought with each other over the issue of money collection during the previous dry season. Since then they would have nothing to do with the deep tubewell.

This struck me as a terrible shame. In a country of famine, here was a 300-foot deep tubewell—a driven well—that could irrigate some sixty acres. I decided to make the tubewell work again.

It was not easy. Of all the modes of irrigation then available, deep tubewells were the most capital intensive. With their high operating costs, they proved highly inefficient and encouraged rampant corruption among those who dealt in fuel oil, lubricants, and spare parts. For the deep tubewell to operate efficiently, it needed an efficient water distribution system. In other words, it required a large number of small farmers to implement uniform crop decisions on their fragmented holdings. These farmers also needed instruction on fertilizer use, plant protection, and the repair and maintenance of the pumps. Unfortunately, although the government generously invested in modern irrigation technology, it did not provide the time, the resources, or the effort to resolve the people-centered problems such technology brought with it. Because of perennial management problems and technical breakdowns, the farmers were reluctant to reopen their tubewells. As a result, almost half the deep tubewells in Bangladesh had fallen out of use. The rusting machinery in abandoned pump houses was a testimony to yet another failure of misguided development.

In Jobra, I called a meeting of local farmers and sharecroppers. I proposed an experiment, in which we would all join a new type of agricultural cooperative called the Nabajug ("New Era") Three Share Farm. The landowners would contribute the use of their land during the dry season; the sharecroppers would contribute their labor; and I would contribute the cost of fuel to run the deep tubewell, the seeds for high-yield crops, the fertilizer, the insecticide, and the technical know-how. In exchange, each of the three parties (farmers, sharecroppers, and myself) would share one-third of the harvest.

At first the villagers were suspicious of my proposal. So much ill will and distrust had built up between the well operators and the farmers that they were not ready to listen to my plan. Some argued that paying me one-third of the harvest would be too much. Even with my offer to bear all losses, my proposal failed to interest them.

At a second meeting, one week later, I was able to convince them that they had nothing to lose. They would receive irrigation water, fertilizer, seeds, and insecticides without any up-front payment. They only had to agree to give me one-third of their harvest. The poor sharecroppers greeted my proposal with enthusiasm. The relatively well-off farmers reluctantly agreed to give it a try.

This was a difficult period for me. I would often lie awake at night, anxious lest anything go wrong. Every Tuesday evening I visited the farmers and held a formal meeting with the four student "block leaders" I had appointed as well as my thirteen-man advisory team. We discussed and reviewed the problems of fertilizer, irrigation, technology, storage, transport, and marketing.

The first year's efforts ended in success. The farmers were happy. They had not spent any cash and had gotten a high yield. I, however, lost 13,000 taka because some farmers gave me less than the one-third they had promised. But I was still thrilled. We had managed to grow a crop where no crop had ever grown before in the dry season. The fields had been full of the emerald green of standing rice. Nothing is quite as beautiful as farmers harvesting their rice. The sight warmed my heart.

■

But I still had misgivings. The success of our three-share experiment had highlighted a problem I had not focused on before. Once the rice was harvested, labor was needed to separate the rice from the dry straw. This mindless, boring work was offered to the cheapest day laborers: destitute women who would otherwise be reduced to begging. For hours on end these poor women would separate the rice with their feet, holding themselves upright by gripping the tiny ledges on the wall in front of them. All day, some twenty-five to thirty women would perform this continuous twisting motion, wrapping the rice straws around their feet to separate the paddy. In the early morning they would race to work, competing for the most comfortable position against the wall. What a terrible life—to earn forty cents investing the weight of your body and the tiresome motion of your bare feet for ten hours a day! These women, many of them widowed, divorced, or abandoned with children to feed, were too poor even to be sharecroppers. They were landless and assetless and without any hope. They were the poorest of the poor. It was clear to me that the wealthier the farmer, the more he earned from my Three Share Farm experiment, and the poorer the worker, the smaller was her share. "Why should we be happy with your Three Share Farm?" one woman said to me. "After a few weeks of threshing, we are out of work, and we have nothing to show for ourselves." She was right. For the same work, a woman could earn at least four times more if she had the financial resources to buy the rice paddy and process it herself.

The more I studied Jobra's poverty, the more I realized how important it was to differentiate between the really poor and the marginal farmers. International development programs in rural areas always focus on farmers and landowners. In Bangladesh, half of the total population is worse off than the marginal farmer. At the time I was studying Jobra, government bureaucrats and social scientists had not clarified who the "poor" in fact were. Back then, "poor person" could mean many things. For some, the term referred to a jobless person, an illiterate person, a landless person, or a homeless person. For others, a poor person was one who could not produce enough food to feed his or her family year-round. Still others thought a poor person was one who owned a thatched house with a rotten roof, who suffered from malnutrition, or who did not send his or her children to school. Such conceptual vagueness greatly damaged our efforts to alleviate poverty. For one thing, most definitions of the poor left out women and children. In my work, I found it useful to use three broad definitions of poor to describe the situation in Bangladesh*:

P1—the bottom 20 percent of the population ("hard-core poor"/absolute poor)

P2—bottom 35 percent of the population

P3—bottom 50 percent of the population

Within each category of poor, I often created subclassifications on the basis of region, occupation, religion, ethnic background, sex, age, and so on. Occupational or regional categories may not be as quantifiable as income-asset criteria, but they help us to create a multidimensional poverty matrix.

Like navigation markings in unknown waters, definitions of poverty need to be distinctive and unambiguous. A definition that is not precise is as bad as no definition at all. In my definition of the poor, I would include the women who threshed rice on our Three Share Farm; women who made bamboo stools: and petty traders who had to borrow at 10 percent per month or sometimes per week. I would also include others like them who earned so little weaving their baskets and sleeping mats that they often resorted to begging. These people had absolutely no chance of improving their economic base. Each one was stuck in poverty.

---

*In 1995, the Consultative Group to Assist the Poorest (CGAP) and the Microcredit Summit Campaign Committee formally defined a "poor" person as someone who lives below the poverty line and "poorest" as someone in the bottom half of those below the poverty line.

■

My experience with Jobra's deep tubewell convinced me to turn my focus on the landless poor. Soon I started arguing that wherever a poverty alleviation program allowed the nonpoor to be co-passengers, the poor would soon be elbowed out of the program by those who were better off. In the world of development, if one mixes the poor and the nonpoor in a program, the nonpoor will always drive out the poor, and the less poor will drive out the more poor, unless protective measures are instituted right at the beginning. In such cases, the nonpoor reap the benefits of all that is done in the name of the poor.

CHAPTER

FOUR

The Stool Makers

of Jobra Village

In 1976, I began visiting the poorest households in Jobra to see if I could help them directly in any way. There were three parts to the village: a Muslim, a Hindu, and a Buddhist section. When I visited the Buddhist section, I would often take one of my students, Dipal Chandra Barua, a native of the Buddhist section, along with me. Otherwise, a colleague, Professor H. I. Latifee, would usually accompany me. He knew most of the families and had a natural talent for making villagers feel at ease.

One day as Latifee and I were making our rounds in Jobra, we stopped at a run-down house with crumbling mud walls and a low thatched roof pocked with holes. We made our way through a crowd of scavenging chickens and beds of vegetables to the front of the house. A woman squatted on the dirt floor of the verandah, a half-finished bamboo stool gripped between her knees. Her fingers moved quickly, plaiting the stubborn strands of cane. She was totally absorbed in her work.

On hearing Latifee's call of greeting, she dropped her bamboo, sprang to her feet, and scurried into the house.

"Don't be frightened," Latifee called out. "We are not strangers. We teach up at the university. We are neighbors. We want to ask you a few questions, that is all."

Reassured by Latifee's gentle manner, she answered in a low voice, "There is nobody home."

She meant there was no male at home. In Bangladesh, women are not supposed to talk to men who are not close relatives.

Children were running around naked in the yard. Neighbors peered out at us from their windows, wondering what we were doing.

In the Muslim sections of Jobra, we often had to talk to women through bamboo walls or curtains. The custom of *purdah* (literally, "curtain" or "veil") kept married Muslim women in a state of virtual seclusion from the outside world. It was strictly observed in Chittagong District.

As I am a native Chittagonian and speak the local dialect, I would try to gain the confidence of Muslim women by chatting. Complimenting a mother on her baby was a natural way to put her at ease. I now picked up one of the naked children beside me, but he started to cry and rushed over to his mother. She let him climb into her arms.

"How many children do you have?" Latifee asked her.

"Three."

"He is very beautiful, this one," I said.

Slightly reassured, the mother came to the doorway, holding her baby. She was in her early twenties, thin, with dark skin and black eyes. She wore a red sari and had the tired eyes of a woman who labored every day from morning to night.

"What is your name?" I asked.

"Sufiya Begum."

"How old are you?"

"Twenty-one."

I did not use a pen and notepad, for that would have scared her off. Later, I only allowed my students to take notes on return visits.

"Do you own this bamboo?" I asked.

"Yes."

"How do you get it?"

"I buy it."

"How much does the bamboo cost you?"

"Five taka." At the time, this was about twenty-two cents.

"Do you have five taka?"

"No, I borrow it from the *paikars*."

"The middlemen? What is your arrangement with them?"

"I must sell my bamboo stools back to them at the end of the day as repayment for my loan."

"How much do you sell a stool for?"

"Five taka and fifty poysha."

"So you make fifty poysha profit?"

She nodded. That came to a profit of just two cents.

"And could you borrow the cash from the moneylender and buy your own raw material?"

"Yes, but the moneylender would demand a lot. People who deal with them only get poorer."

"How much does the moneylender charge?"

"It depends. Sometimes he charges 10 percent per week. But I have one neighbor who is paying 10 percent per day."

"And that is all you earn from making these beautiful bamboo stools, fifty poysha?"

"Yes."

Sufiya did not want to waste any more time talking. I watched as she set to work again, her small brown hands plaiting the strands of bamboo as they had every day for months and years on end. This was her livelihood. She squatted barefoot on the hard mud. Her fingers were callused, her nails black with grime.

How would her children break the cycle of poverty she had started? How could they go to school when the income Sufiya earned was barely enough to feed her, let alone shelter her family and clothe them properly? It seemed hopeless to imagine that her babies would one day escape this misery.

Sufiya Begum earned two cents a day. It was this knowledge that shocked me. In my university courses, I theorized about sums in the millions of dollars, but here before my eyes the problems of life and death were posed in terms of pennies. Something was wrong. Why did my university courses not reflect the reality of Sufiya's life? I was angry, angry at myself, angry at my economics department and the thousands of intelligent professors who had not tried to address this problem and solve it. It seemed to me the existing economic system made it absolutely certain that Sufiya's income would be kept perpetually at such a low level that she would never save a penny and would never invest in expanding her economic base. Her children were condemned to live a life of penury, of hand-to-mouth survival, just as she had lived it before them, and as her parents did before her. I had never heard of anyone suffering for the lack of *twenty-two cents*. It seemed impossible to me, preposterous. Should I reach into my pocket and hand Sufiya the pittance she needed for capital? That would be so simple, so easy. I resisted the urge to give Sufiya the money she needed. She was not asking for charity. And giving one person twenty-two cents was not addressing the problem on any permanent basis.

Latifee and I drove back up the hill to my house. We took a stroll around my garden in the late-afternoon heat. I was trying to see Sufiya's problem from her point of view. She suffered because the cost of the bamboo was five taka. She did not have the cash necessary to buy her raw materials. As a result, she could survive only in a tight cycle—borrowing from the trader and selling back to him. Her life was a form of bonded labor, or slavery. The trader made certain that he paid Sufiya a price that barely covered the cost of the materials and was just enough to keep her alive. She could not break free of her exploitative relationship with him. To survive, she needed to keep working through the trader.

Usurious rates have become so standardized and socially acceptable in Third World countries that the borrower rarely realizes how oppressive a contract is. Exploitation comes in many guises. In rural Bangladesh, one *maund* (approximately 37 kilograms) of husked rice borrowed at the beginning of the planting season has to be repaid with two *maunds* at harvest time. When land is used as security, it is placed at the disposal of the creditor, who enjoys ownership rights over it until the total amount is repaid. In many cases, a formal document such as a *bawnanama* establishes the right of the creditor. According to the *bawnanama*, the creditor usually refuses to accept any partial payment of the loan. After the expiration of a certain period, it also allows the creditor to "buy" the land at a predetermined "price." Another form of security is the *dadan* system, in which traders advance loans against standing crops for purchase of the crops at predetermined prices that are below the market rate. Sufiya Begum was producing her bamboo stools under a *dadan* arrangement with a *paikar*.

In Bangladesh, the borrowing is sometimes made for specific and temporary purposes (to marry off a daughter, to bribe an official, to fight a court case), but sometimes it is necessary for physical survival—to purchase food or medication or to meet some emergency situation. In such cases, it is extremely difficult for the borrower to extricate himself or herself from the burden of the loan. Usually the borrower will have to borrow again just to repay the prior loan and will ultimately wind up in a cycle of poverty like Sufiya. It seemed to me that Sufiya's status as a bonded slave would only change if she could find that five taka for her bamboo. Credit could bring her that money. She could then sell her products in a free market and charge the full retail price to the consumer. She just needed twenty-two cents.

The next day I called in Maimuna Begum, a university student who collected data for me, and asked her to help me make a list of people in Jobra, like Sufiya, who were dependent on traders. Within one week, we had a list prepared. It named forty-two people, who borrowed a total of 856 taka–less than 27 dollars.

"My God, my God. All this misery in all these families all for of the lack of twenty-seven dollars!" I exclaimed.

Maimuna stood there without saying a word. We were both sickened by the reality of it all.

My mind would not let this problem lie. I wanted to help these forty-two able-bodied, hard-working people. I kept going around and around the problem, like a dog worrying a bone. People like Sufiya were poor not because they were stupid or lazy. They worked all day long, doing complex physical tasks. They were poor because the financial institutions in the country did not help them widen their economic base. No formal financial structure was available to cater to the credit needs of the poor. This credit market, by default of the formal institutions, had been taken over by the local moneylenders. It was an efficient vehicle; it created a heavy rush of one-way traffic on the road to poverty. But if I could just lend the Jobra villagers the twenty-seven dollars, they could sell their products to anyone. They would then get the highest possible return for their labor and would not be limited by the usurious practices of the traders and moneylenders.

It was all so easy. I handed Maimuna the twenty-seven dollars and told her, "Here, lend this money to the forty-two villagers on our list. They can repay the traders what they owe them and sell their products at a good price."

"When should they repay you?" she asked.

"Whenever they can," I said. "Whenever it is advantageous for them to sell their products. They don't have to pay any interest. I am not in the money business."

Maimuna left, puzzled by this turn of events.

■

Usually when my head touches the pillow, I fall asleep within seconds, but that night sleep would not come. I lay in bed feeling ashamed that I was part of a society that could not provide twenty-seven dollars to forty-two skilled persons to make a living for themselves. It struck me that what I had done was drastically insufficient. If others needed capital, they could hardly chase down the head of an economics department. My response had been ad hoc and emotional. Now I needed to create an institutional answer that these people could rely on. What was required was an institution that would lend to those who had nothing. I decided to approach the local bank manager and request that his bank lend money to the poor. It seemed so simple, so straightforward. I fell asleep.

The next morning I climbed into my white Volkswagen beetle and drove to my local branch of the Janata Bank, a government bank and one of the largest in the country. Janata's university branch is located just beyond the gates of the campus on a stretch of road lined with tiny stores, stalls, and restaurants where local villagers sell students everything from betel nuts to warm meals, notebooks, and pens. It is here that the rickshaw drivers congregate when they are not ferrying students from their dormitories to their classrooms. The bank itself is housed in a single square room. Its two front windows are covered with bars and the walls are painted a dingy dark green. The room is filled with wooden tables and chairs. The manager, sitting in the back to the left, waved me over.

"What can I do for you, sir?"

The office boy brought us tea and cookies. I explained why I had come. "The last time I borrowed from you was to finance the Three Share Program in Jobra village. Now I have a new proposal. I want you to lend money to the poor people in Jobra. The amount involved is very small. I have already done it myself. I have lent twenty-seven dollars to forty-two people. There will be many more poor people who will need money. They need this money to carry on their work, to buy raw materials and supplies."

"What kind of materials?" The bank officer looked puzzled, as if this were some sort of new game whose rules he was not familiar with. He let me speak out of common respect for a university head, but he was clearly confused.

"Well, some make bamboo stools. Others weave mats or drive rickshaws. If they borrow money from a bank at commercial rates, they will be able to sell their products on the open market and make a decent profit that would allow them to live better lives. As it is now, they work as slaves and will never manage to get themselves out from under the heel of the wholesalers who lend them capital at usurious rates."

"Yes, I know about *mahajons* [moneylenders]," the manager replied.

"So I have come here today because I would like to ask you to lend money to these villagers."

The bank manager's jaw fell open, and he started to laugh. "I can't do that!"

"Why not?" I asked.

"Well," he sputtered, not knowing where to begin with his list of objections. "For one thing, the small amounts you say these villagers need to borrow will not even cover the cost of all the loan documents they would have to fill out. The bank is not going to waste its time on such a pittance."

"Why not?" I said. "To the poor this money is crucial for survival."

"These people are illiterate," he replied. "They cannot even fill out our loan forms."

"In Bangladesh, where 75 percent of the people do not read and write, filling out a form is a ridiculous requirement."

"Every single bank in the country has that rule."

"Well, that says something about our banks then, doesn't it?"

"Even when a person brings money and wants to put it in the bank, we ask him or her to write down how much she or he is putting in."

"Why?"

"What do you mean, 'Why?'"

"Well, why can't a bank just take money and issue a receipt saying, 'Received such and such amount of money from such and such a person?' Why can't the banker do it? Why must the depositors do it?"

"Well, how would you run a bank without people reading and writing?"

"Simple, the bank just issues a receipt for the amount of cash that the bank receives."

"What if the person wants to withdraw money?"

"I don't know . . . there must be a simple way. The borrower comes back with his or her deposit receipt, presents it to the cashier, and the cashier gives back the money. Whatever accounting the bank does is the bank's business."

The manager shook his head but did not answer this, as if he did not know where to begin.

"It seems to me your banking system is designed to be anti-illiterate," I countered.

Now the branch manager seemed irritated. "Professor, banking is not as simple as you think," he said.

"Maybe so, but I am also sure that banking is not as complicated as you make it out to be."

"Look, the simple truth is that a borrower at any other bank in any place in the world would have to fill out forms."

"Okay," I said, bowing to the obvious. "If I can get some of my student volunteers to fill out the forms for the villagers, that should not be a problem."

"But you don't understand, we simply cannot lend to the destitute," said the branch manager.

"Why not?" I was trying to be polite. Our conversation had something surreal about it. The branch manager had a smile on his face as if to say he understood that I was pulling his leg. This whole interview was humorous, absurd really.

"They don't have any collateral," said the branch manager, expecting that this would put an end to our discussion.

"Why do you need collateral as long as you get the money back? That is what you really want, isn't it?"

"Yes, we want our money back," explained the manager. "But at the same time we need collateral. That is our guarantee."

"To me, it doesn't make sense. The poorest of the poor work twelve hours a day. They need to sell and earn income to eat. They have every reason to pay you back, just to take another loan and live another day! That is the best security you can have—their life."

The manager shook his head. "You are an idealist, Professor. You live with books and theories."

"But if you are certain that the money will be repaid, why do you need collateral?"

"That is our bank rule."

"So only those who have collateral can borrow?"

"Yes."

"It's a silly rule. It means only the rich can borrow."

"I don't make the rules, the bank does."

"Well, I think the rules should be changed."

"Anyway, we do not lend out money here."

"You don't?"

"No, we only take deposits from the faculty members and from the university."

"But don't banks make money by extending loans?"

"Only the head office makes loans. We are here to collect deposits from the university and its employees. Our loan to your Three Share Farm was an exception approved by our head office."

"You mean to say that if I came here and asked to borrow money, you would not lend it to me?"

"That is right." He laughed. It was evident the manager had not had such an entertaining afternoon in a long time.

"So when we teach in our classes that banks make loans to borrowers, that is a lie?"

"Well, you would have to go through the head office for a loan, and I don't know what they would do."

"Sounds like I need to talk to officials higher up."

"Yes, that would be a good idea."

As I finished my tea and got ready to leave, the branch manager said, "I know you'll not give up. But from what I know about banking, I can tell you for sure that this plan of yours will never take off."

A couple of days later, I arranged a meeting with Mr. R. A. Howladar, the regional manager of the Janata Bank, in his office in Chittagong. We had very much a repeat of the conversation I had with the Jobra branch manager, but Howladar did bring up the idea of a guarantor, a well-to-do person in the village who would be willing to act on behalf of the borrower. With the backing of a guarantor, the bank might consider granting a loan without collateral.

I considered the idea. It had obvious merit, but the drawbacks seemed insurmountable.

"I can't do that," I explained to Howladar. "What would prevent the guarantor from taking advantage of the person whose loan he was guaranteeing? He could end up a tyrant. He could end up treating that borrower as a slave."

There was a silence. It had become clear from my discussions with bankers in the past few days that I was not up against the Janata Bank per se but against the banking system in general.

"Why don't I become guarantor?" I asked.

"You?"

"Yes, can you accept me as guarantor for all the loans?"

The regional manager smiled. "How much money are you talking about?"

To give myself a margin of error and room to expand, I answered, "Altogether probably 10,000 taka ($300), not more than that."

"Well," he fingered the papers on his desk. Behind him I could see a dusty stack of folders in old bindings. Lining the walls were piles of similar pale blue binders, rising in teetering stacks to the windows. The overhead fan created a breeze that played with the files. On his desk, the papers were in a state of permanent fluttering, awaiting his decision.

"Well," he said. "I would say we would be willing to accept you as guarantor up to that amount, but don't ask for more money."

"It's a deal."

We shook hands. Then something occurred to me. "But if one of the borrowers does not repay, I will not step in to honor the defaulted loan."

The regional manager looked up at me uneasily, not certain why I was being so difficult.

"As guarantor, we could force you to pay."

"What would you do?"

"We could start legal proceedings against you."

"Fine. I would like that."

He looked at me as if I were crazy. That was just what I wanted. I felt angry. I wanted to cause some panic in this unjust, archaic system. I wanted to be the stick in the wheels that would finally stop this infernal machine. I was a guarantor, maybe, but I would not guarantee.

"Professor Yunus, you know very well we would never sue a department head who has personally guaranteed the loan of a beggar. The bad publicity alone would offset any money we might recover from you. Anyway, the loan is such a pittance it would not even pay for the legal fees, much less our administrative costs of recovering the money."

"Well, you are a bank, you must do your own cost-benefit analysis. But I will not pay if there is any default."

"You are making things difficult for me, Professor Yunus."

"I am sorry, but the bank is making things difficult for a lot of people—especially those who have nothing."

"I am trying to help, Professor."

"I understand. It is not you but banking rules I have a quarrel with."

After more such back and forth, Howladar concluded, "I will recommend your loan to the head office in Dhaka, and we will see what they say."

"But I thought you as regional officer had the authority to conclude this matter?"

"Yes, but this is far too unorthodox for me to approve. Authorization will have to come from the top."

■

It took six months of writing back and forth to get the loan formalized. Finally, in December 1976, I succeeded in taking out a loan from the Janata Bank and giving it to the poor of Jobra. All through 1977, I had to sign each and every loan request. Even when I was on a trip in Europe or the United States, the bank would cable or write to me for a signature rather than deal with any of the real borrowers in the village. I was the guarantor and as far as the bank officials were concerned I was the only one that counted. They did not want to deal with the poor who used their capital. And I made sure that the real borrowers, the ones I call the "banking untouchables," never had to suffer the indignity and demeaning harassment of actually going to a bank.

That was the beginning of it all. I never intended to become a moneylender. I had no intention of lending money to anyone. All I really wanted was to solve an immediate problem. Out of sheer frustration, I had questioned the most basic banking premise of collateral. I did not know if I was right. I had no idea what I was getting myself into. I was walking blind and learning as I went along. My work became a struggle to show that the financial untouchables are actually touchable, even huggable. To my great surprise, the repayment of loans by people who borrow without collateral has proven to be much better than those whose borrowings are secured by assets. Indeed, more than 98 percent of our loans are repaid. The poor know that this credit is their only opportunity to break out of poverty. They do not have any cushion whatsoever to fall back on. If they fall afoul of this one loan, they will have lost their one and only chance to get out of the rut.

A Pilot Project Is Born

I did not know anything about how to run a bank for the poor, so I had to learn from scratch. In January 1977, when Grameen started, I studied how others ran their loan operations and I learned from their mistakes. Conventional banks and credit cooperatives usually demand lump sum payments. Parting with a large amount of cash at the end of a loan period is often psychologically trying for borrowers. They try to delay the repayment as long as they can and in the process they make the loan grow bigger and bigger. In the end, they decide not to pay back the loan at all. Such long-term lump sum payments also prompt both borrowers and lenders to ignore difficulties that come up early on; rather than tackle problems as they appear, they hope that the problems will go away by the time the loan is due.

In structuring our credit program, I decided to do exactly the opposite of traditional banks. To overcome the psychological barrier of parting with large sums, I decided to institute a daily payment program. I made the loan payments so small that borrowers would barely miss the money. And for ease in accounting, I decided to ask that the loans be paid back fully in one year. Thus, a 365 taka loan could be paid at the rate of 1 taka a day over the course of one year.

To most of those who will read this book, a taka a day may seem like a laughable sum, but it does produce steady incremental gains. The power of the daily taka reminds me of the clever prisoner who was condemned to death. Brought before the king on his execution day, the prisoner was granted one last wish. He pointed to the chessboard at the right of the king's throne and said, "I wish only for a single grain of rice on one square of the chessboard and that that grain be doubled for each succeeding square."

"Granted," said the king, who could not fathom the power of geometrical progression. Soon the prisoner reigned over the entire kingdom.

■

Slowly my colleagues and I developed our own delivery-recovery mechanism and, of course, we made many mistakes along the way. We adapted our ideas and changed our procedures as we grew. For example, when we discovered that support groups were crucial to the success of our operations, we required that each applicant join a group of like-minded people living in similar economic and social conditions. Convinced that solidarity would be stronger if the groups came into being by themselves, we refrained from managing them, but we did create incentives that encouraged the borrowers to help one another succeed in their businesses. Group membership not only creates support and protection but also smooths out the erratic behavior patterns of individual members, making each borrower more reliable in the process. Subtle and at times not-so-subtle peer pressure keeps each group member in line with the broader objectives of the credit program. A sense of intergroup and intragroup competition also encourages each member to be an achiever. Shifting the task of initial supervision to the group not only reduces the work of the bank but also increases the self-reliance of the individual borrowers. Because the group approves the loan request of each member, the group assumes moral responsibility for the loan. If any member of the group gets into trouble, the group usually comes forward to help.

In Jobra, we discovered that it is not always easy for borrowers to organize themselves into groups. A prospective borrower first has to take the initiative and explain how the bank works to a second person. This can be particularly difficult for a village woman. She often has a difficult time convincing her friends—who are likely to be terrified, skeptical, or forbidden by their husbands to deal with money—but eventually a second person, impressed by what Grameen has done for another household, will take the leap of joining the group. Then the two will go out and seek out a third member, then a fourth, and a fifth. Once the group of five is formed, we extend loans to two members of the group. If these two repay regularly for the next six weeks, two more members may request loans. The chairperson of the group is normally the last borrower of the five. But often, just when the group is ready, one of the five members changes her mind, saying, "No, my husband won't agree. He doesn't want me to join the bank." So the group falls back to four, or three, or sometimes back to one. And that one has to start all over again.

It can take anywhere from a few days to several months for a group to be recognized or certified by Grameen Bank. To gain recognition, all the members of a group of five prospective borrowers have to present themselves to the bank, undergo at least seven days of training on our policies, and demonstrate their understanding of those policies in an oral examination administered by a senior bank official. Each of the members must be individually tested. The night before her test, a borrower often gets so nervous that she lights a candle in a saint's shrine and prays to Allah for help. She knows that if she fails she will let down not only herself but also the others in her group. Though she has studied, she worries that she will not be able to answer the questions about the duties and responsibilities of a Grameen Bank member. What if she forgets? The bank worker will send the group away, telling all the members to study some more, and the others in the group will chastise her, saying, "For God's sake, even this you can't do right! You have ruined not only yourself but us as well."

Some critics argue that our rural clients are too submissive and that we can intimidate them into joining Grameen. Perhaps this is why we make our initiation process so challenging. The pressure provided by the group and the exam helps ensure that only those who are truly needy and serious about joining Grameen will actually become members. Those who are better off usually do not find it worthwhile. And even if they do, they will fail our means test and be forced to leave the group anyway. We want only courageous, ambitious pioneers in our micro-credit program. Those are the ones who will succeed.

Once all members pass the exam, the day finally comes when one of them asks for a first loan, usually about twenty-five dollars, in the eighties. How does she feel? Terrified. She cannot sleep at night. She struggles with the fear of failure, the fear of the unknown. The morning she is to receive her loan, she almost quits. Twenty-five dollars is simply too much responsibility for her. How will she ever be able to repay it? No woman in her extended family has ever had so much money. Her friends come around to reassure her, saying, "Look, we all have to go through it. We will support you. We are here for just that. Don't be scared. We will all be with you."

When she finally receives the twenty-five dollars, she is trembling. The money burns her fingers. Tears roll down her face. She has never seen so much money in her life. She never imagined it in her hands. She carries the bills as she would a delicate bird or a rabbit, until someone advises her to put the money away in a safe place lest it be stolen.

This is the beginning for almost every Grameen borrower. All her life she has been told that she is no good, that she brings only misery to her family, and that they cannot afford to pay her dowry. Many times she hears her mother or her father tell her she should have been killed at birth, aborted, or starved. To her family she has been nothing but another mouth to feed, another dowry to pay. But today, for the first time in her life, an institution has trusted her with a great sum of money. She promises that she will never let down the institution or herself. She will struggle to make sure that every penny is paid back.

■

Early on, we encouraged our borrowers to build up savings that they could fall back on in hard times or use for additional income-generating opportunities. We required all borrowers to deposit 5 percent of each loan in a group fund. They understood this tactic as being similar to the Bengali custom of *mushti chal* ("handful of rice"), where a housewife puts away small amounts of rice every day to slowly build up a substantial reserve. Any borrower can take an interest-free loan from the group fund,* provided that all the other members of the group approve of the amount and its usage and that the loan does not exceed half of the fund's total. In thousands of cases each year, loans made to our members from their group funds stave off seasonal malnutrition, pay for medical treatments, purchase school supplies, recapitalize businesses affected by natural disasters, and finance modest but dignified family burials. As of 1998, the total amount in all the group funds exceeded $100 million—more than the net worth of all but a handful of Bangladeshi companies.

If an individual is unable or unwilling to pay back her loan, her group may become ineligible for larger loans in subsequent years until the repayment problem is brought under control. This cre-

*Under Grameen II, group fund has been replaced by individual savings.

ates a powerful incentive for borrowers to help each other solve problems and—even more important—to *prevent* problems. Groups can also request help from other groups in their "center," a federation of up to eight groups in a village that meets weekly with a bank worker at a predetermined place and time. A center chief, a group chairperson who is elected by all members to manage the center's affairs, helps solve any problems that a group is unable to handle on its own and works closely with the bank worker assigned to the center. The chief also plays an active role in screening loan requests. When a member makes a formal loan request during a meeting, the bank worker will normally ask the group chairperson and the center chief whether they support the loan proposal—both the amount and its purpose.

From the very beginning, we decided that all business conducted during center meetings should be done out in the open. This reduced the danger of corruption, mismanagement, and misunderstandings and it kept the leaders and the bank workers directly accountable to the borrowers. Often borrowers would invite their children to join the meetings before school, so that these young ones could read them the notations in their passbooks and make sure that everything was being done correctly.

I still find it exciting to travel out to Grameen villages and meet with centers. With each passing year the borrowers assume more responsibilities for the management of their own affairs. They come up with more innovative approaches to preventing and solving problems and find new ways to ensure that each member rises above the poverty line as quickly as possible. I always return from the villages more convinced that providing credit is a powerful means to create profound change in people's lives. It has been that way since I started visiting centers in 1977 and continues to this day. When I visit center meetings, not only in Bangladesh but all over the world, in countries as diverse as Malaysia, the Philippines, South Africa, and the United States, I realize how resilient and creative human beings can be when given the chance.

One example of resilience is Mufia Khatoon, a Grameen borrower from Mirsharai District, north of Chittagong. Mufia joined Grameen in late 1979. Her life had been filled with sorrow until that point. In 1963, at the age of thirteen, she was married by her father, a kind-hearted farmer and fisherman, to a man named Jamiruddin of Dom Khali village in Mirsharai. During her husband's long absences at sea on a fishing boat, Mufia's mother-in-law verbally abused her and made sure she received little if any food even after doing all the cooking. Mufia lived a half-starved existence for years. When her husband returned home, he often beat Mufia. Occasionally her father, who lived a few miles away, tried to protect her, but his efforts made no lasting impact on how she was treated.

Mufia became pregnant three times during these years, but one child died shortly after birth, and she was unable to carry the other two to term. Suffering from malnutrition and anemia, she finally gave birth to a son who survived, but it left her in a precarious state of health. Somehow she recovered, but the beatings and the life of semistarvation continued.

In 1974, a village leader intervened and arranged for a divorce. Mufia was then free from her husband's beatings, but starvation followed her into her new life. She began begging. She begged in the rich neighborhoods of Khaiachara and Mithachara villages. An entire day's begging would yield a few ounces of rice, hardly enough for her and her three children (after her son, she had two daughters, and she also looked after a nephew who was an orphan). One day she was begging from a woman who had a home-based business making baskets, mats, and other items from bamboo. She asked Mufia if she would want to borrow fifteen taka from her to buy some bamboo and sell it in the market. Mufia agreed, made a ten taka profit, and repaid the loan. With the ten taka, she bought some food for her family. This was repeated a few times over the next few years, but after a while the woman stopped giving Mufia loans and she was forced to become a full-time beggar again.

Mufia starved through the famine of 1974 and her makeshift house was destroyed in a storm in 1978. But in 1979, she joined the Grameen Bank and borrowed 500 taka to restart her bamboo business. When she paid back her first loan, she felt like a new person. Her second loan, received on December 25, 1980, was for 1,500 taka. Although she sometimes missed installments during the lean season when demand for bamboo products was low, she always caught up when the economy improved after the rice harvest.

During her first eighteen months as a Grameen Bank member, Mufia was able to buy 330 taka worth of clothing for herself and her children and cookware for 105 taka. These were luxuries that she had not had since she was divorced from her husband fifteen years earlier. She and her children were also eating more regularly and more nutritious food. Meat was never an option, but vegetables were more common, and occasionally she bought dried fish in the market as a treat.

Mufia is one of thousands of former beggars who are now living a dignified life because they were able to access loans from Grameen Bank. To help inexperienced borrowers like Mufia, we have always tried to simplify our lending operations. Today we have distilled our repayment mechanism to the following formula:

- Loans last one year.

- Installments are paid weekly.

- Repayment starts one week after the loan.

- The interest rate is 20 percent.

- Repayment amounts to 2 percent of the loan amount per week for fifty weeks.

- Interest payments amount to 2 taka per week for every 1,000 taka of the loan amount.

As for the repayment mechanism, I decided that we should keep it as simple as possible. I felt that the transaction should be local, and so in Jobra village I went to visit the *pan* (betel leaf) seller in his tiny stall in the middle of the village. A small man with a toothy grin and unshaven face, he kept his shop open day and night, and he knew just about everyone in the village. Certainly everyone knew him. When I suggested that he be the collection point for Jobra, he was enthusiastic. He did not ask for any fee. We told the borrowers that every day as they cross the road or go about their ordinary business, they should simply give their daily installment to the *pan* seller.

This proved to be a short-lived experiment. Borrowers claimed they had paid their daily installment, and the *pan* seller said they had not.

"Don't you remember?" a borrower would say. "I came at midday. I bought some *pan* from you. I gave you five taka, and when you gave me my change I told you keep my installment of loan repayment. Don't you remember?"

"No, you didn't give me five taka."

"Yes, I did. I remember it very well."

"No, you paid me with a bill and I gave you back full change."

Arguments were unending. I knew we had to simplify the procedure. So I bought a notebook, and on the left I wrote each borrower's name. In the center I made three columns showing amounts paid per installment and the date:

Name of Borrower   Installment Amount   Date

I made the sheet simple so that the *pan* seller needed only to make a check mark each time a borrower paid him. But after a few days even this system broke down. The borrowers claimed that the *pan* seller had forgotten to check them off. Something had to be done about my accounting system. But what? As an experiment, I abandoned the daily repayment system and moved to the next best thing, a weekly repayment system. Today, some twenty years later, our loans are still paid in the same way, week by week, though now they are made to our frontline bank workers who meet weekly with borrowers in their villages.

Our repayment rate has remained high all along. Generally, it is our success in getting high repayment while serving very poor people in disaster-prone areas that surprises people the most about Grameen's success. People sometimes assume that faithful repayment of loans must be part of Bangladeshi "culture." But nothing could be further from the truth. In Bangladesh, the wealthiest borrowers make it a habit not to pay back their loans. I am amazed by the mockery that goes on in the name of banking. Public deposits go through the banking system, through the government banks, through private banks, to people who will never pay back the money.

If Grameen was to work, we knew we had to trust our clients. From day one, we knew that there would be no room for policing in our system. We never used courts to settle our repayments. We did not involve lawyers or any outsiders. Today, commercial banks assume that every borrower is going to run away with their money, so they tie their clients up in legal knots. Lawyers pore over their precious documents, making certain that no borrower will escape the reach of the bank. In contrast, Grameen assumes that every borrower is honest. There are no legal instruments between the lenders and the borrowers. We were convinced that the bank should be built on human trust, not on meaningless paper contracts. Grameen would succeed or fail depending on the strength of our personal relationships. We may be accused of being naive, but our experience with bad debt is less than 1 percent. And even when borrowers do default on a loan, we do not assume that they are malevolent. Instead, we assume that personal circumstances have prevented them from repaying the money. Bad loans present a constant reminder of the need to do more to help our clients succeed.

While we struggled to develop an effective and reliable credit delivery and recovery mechanism during our pilot phase, we also worked on making sure that women benefited from the program. We set a goal of having half of our borrowers be women. This took us more than six years to achieve. In trying to attract woman borrowers, we fought against the normal practices of Bangladeshi banks, which effectively exclude women. To say that our financial institutions are gender-biased is an understatement. When I point out the gender bias of banks, my banker friends grow irritated with me. "Don't you see our ladies' branches all over town?" they argue. "They are designed to serve women only."

"Yes," I answer, "I see them, and I also see the idea behind them. You want to get women's deposits. That is why you make ladies' branches. But what happens when one of the ladies wants to borrow money from you?"

In Bangladesh, if a woman, even a rich woman, wants to borrow money from a bank, the manager will ask her, 'Did you discuss this with your husband?' And if she answers, 'Yes,' the manager will say, 'Is he supportive of your proposal?' If the answer is still, 'Yes,' he will say, 'Would you please bring your husband along so that we can discuss it with him?' But no manager would ever ask a prospective male borrower whether he has discussed the idea of a loan with his wife or whether he would bring his wife along to discuss the proposal. It is not by chance that women constituted less than 1 percent of all the borrowers in Bangladesh prior to Grameen. The banking system was created for men.

It was my anger about this situation that initially prompted me to commit to having at least 50 percent of our experimental project loans granted to women. But we soon discovered new socioeconomic reasons to focus on women. The more money we lent to poor women, the more I realized that credit given to a woman brings about change faster than when given to a man.

In Bangladesh, hunger and poverty are more women's issues than men's. Women experience hunger and poverty more intensely than men. If one of the family members has to starve, it is an unwritten law that it will be the mother. The mother will also suffer the traumatic experience of not being able to breast-feed her infant during the times of famine and scarcity. Poor women in Bangladesh have the most insecure social standing. A husband can throw his wife out any time he wishes. He can divorce her merely by repeating, "I divorce thee," three times. And if he does, she will be disgraced and unwanted in her parents' house. Despite these adversities, it is evident that destitute women adapt quicker and better to the self-help process than men. Though they cannot read or write and have rarely been allowed to step out of their homes alone, poor women see further and are willing to work harder to lift themselves and their families out of poverty. They pay more attention, prepare their children to live better lives, and are more consistent in their performance than men. When a destitute mother starts earning an income, her dreams of success invariably center around her children. A woman's second priority is the household. She wants to buy utensils, build a stronger roof, or find a bed for herself and her family. A man has an entirely different set of priorities. When a destitute father earns extra income, he focuses more attention on himself. Thus money entering a household through a woman brings more benefits to the family as a whole.

If the goals of economic development include improving the general standard of living, reducing poverty, creating dignified employment opportunities, and reducing inequality, then it is natural to work through women. Not only do women constitute the majority of the poor, the underemployed, and the economically and socially disadvantaged, but they more readily and successfully improve the welfare of both children and men. Studies comparing how male borrowers use their loans versus female borrowers, consistently show this to be the case.

It was not easy to focus our efforts almost exclusively on lending to women. The first and most formidable opposition came from the husbands, who generally wanted the loans for themselves. The religious leaders were very suspicious of us. And the moneylenders saw us as a direct threat to their authority in the village. These objections I had expected, but what surprised me was to hear educated civil servants and professionals arguing against us. They contended that it made no sense to lend money to women while so many men were jobless and without income. Or they argued that women would only pass the loans on to their husbands and would wind up even more exploited than they were before. One official of our central bank even wrote me a menacing letter demanding that I "explain fully and immediately why a high percentage of your borrowers are women." Curiously, my reply asking whether the central bank had ever asked the other banks in the country why they have such a high percentage of male borrowers went unanswered.

In the beginning, we were unsure how to attract women borrowers. Bengali women rarely, if ever, borrow money from banks. I could have put up a billboard saying:

ATTENTION ALL WOMEN:

WELCOME TO OUR BANK

FOR A SPECIAL LOAN PROGRAM

FOR WOMEN

This billboard might have received media coverage or free publicity but would never have attracted women borrowers. First, 85 percent of poor women in rural Bangladesh cannot read, and second, they are rarely free to come out of their houses without their husbands. We had to devise a whole series of tricks and techniques to recruit women borrowers. At first, because of the rules of *purdah,* those of us who were men never dared enter a woman's house in the village. *Purdah* refers to a range of practices that uphold the Koranic injunction to guard women's modesty and purity. In its most conservative interpretation, *purdah* forbids women to leave their homes or to be seen by any men except their closest male relatives.

In rural villages like Jobra, *purdah* is colored by beliefs in spirits that predate Islam. Such beliefs are usually perpetuated by the village pseudo-mullahs who teach religious primary schools, or *maktabs,* and interpret Islam for the villagers. Though these men are looked on as religious authorities by the illiterate villagers, many of them have a low degree of Islamic education and do not always base their teachings on the Quran.

Even where *purdah* is not strictly observed, custom, family, tradition, and decorum combine to keep relations between women and men in rural Bangladesh extremely formal. So when I would go to meet with village women, I never asked for a chair or any of the bowing and scraping that usually accompanies figures of authority. Instead, I would try to chat as informally as possible. I would say funny things to break the ice or compliment a mother on her children. I also warned my students and coworkers against wearing expensive dress or fancy saris.

Instead of asking to enter a woman's house, I would stand in a clearing between several houses, so everyone could see me and observe my behavior. Then I would wait while one of my female students entered the appointed house and introduced me. This go-between would then bring me any questions the women might have. I would answer their questions, and back into the house the student would go. Sometimes she would shuttle back and forth for over an hour and still I was not able to convince these hidden women to seek a loan from Grameen.

But I would come back the next day. And again the go-between would shuttle back and forth between the village women and me.

We wasted a lot of time with the student having to repeat every-thing I said and all the questions of the village women. Often our go-between could not catch all my ideas or the women's questions would get jumbled. Sometimes the husbands would get irritated with me. I suppose the fact that I was a respected head of a univer-sity department reassured them somewhat, but always they de-manded that our loans be given to them, not to their wives.

One day, as I sat in a clearing between the houses of a village, it clouded over and started to rain. As this was during the monsoon season, the rain turned into a heavy downpour. The women in the house sent an umbrella out so I could cover myself. I was relatively dry, but the poor go-between got rained on every time she shut-tled back and forth between me and the house. As the rain in-creased one of the elder women in the house, said, "Let the professor take shelter next door. There is no one there. That way the girl won't get wet."

The house was a typical rural Bengali hut—a tiny room with a dirt floor and no electricity, chair, or table. I sat alone on the bed in the dark and waited. Wonderful smells of simmering *atap* rice seeped into the hut from next door. A bamboo wall and cabinets divided this house from the neighboring one, and every time my go-between talked to the women in the adjoining house, I could hear some of the things they said, but their voices were muffled. And every time the go-between would return to tell me what they had said, the women next door would crowd against the bamboo divide to hear my answers. It was far from an ideal way of commu-nicating, but it was certainly better than standing outside in the rain.

After twenty minutes of this—hearing each other's voices, but talking indirectly through a go-between—the women on the other side of the wall started bypassing my assistant and shouting ques-tions or comments directly at me in their Chittagonian dialect. As my eyes grew accustomed to the darkness, I could make out human shapes staring at me through the cracks in the partition. Many of their questions were similar to the ones the men asked us: "Why must we form a group?" "Why not an individual loan to me right now?"

There were about twenty-five women peeking at me through the cracks in the bamboo when suddenly the pressure on the partition grew too great and part of it collapsed. Before they knew what had happened, the women were sitting in the room listening and talking directly to me. Some hid their faces behind a veil. Others giggled and were too shy to look at me directly. But we had no more need of someone to repeat our words. That was the first time I spoke with a group of Jobra women indoors.

"Your words frighten us, sir," one woman said hiding her face with the end of her sari.

"Money is something that only my husband handles," said another, turning her back to me so I could not look at her directly.

"Give the loan to my husband. He handles the money. I've never touched any and I don't want to," said a third.

"I wouldn't know what to do with money," said a woman who sat closest to me but averted her eyes.

"No, no, not me. We have no use for money," said an elderly woman. "We have all had enough trouble with dowry payments and we don't want another fight with our husbands. Professor, we just don't want to get into more trouble."

It was easy to see the crushing effects of poverty and abuse in these faces. As they had no power over anyone else, their husbands would vent their frustrations on these women by beating them. In many ways, the women were treated like animals. I knew that marital violence was a terrible problem and understood why none of these women wanted to get involved in an area reserved traditionally for men—the control of cash.

Still, I tried my best to encourage them not to be afraid. "Why not borrow? It would help you to start earning money."

"No, no, no, we cannot take your money."

"Why not? If you invest it, you can earn money and use the prof-its to feed your children and send them to school."

"No, when my mother died, the last advice she gave me was never to borrow from anybody. So I can't borrow."

"Yes, your mother was a wise woman, she gave you the right ad-vice. But if she were alive today she would advise you to join Grameen. When she was alive, there was no Grameen project. She didn't know anything about this experiment. Back then, there was only one source she could borrow from, the moneylender, and she was advising you rightly not to go to him because he charges 10 percent interest per month or more. But if your mother had known about us, she would definitely have recommended that you join us and make a decent living for yourself."

I had heard their arguments so many times that I had ready an-swers, but it was difficult to persuade these frightened creatures. They had never interacted with any institution in their lives. Every-thing that I offered them was strange and threatening. Progress was slow that day. Very slow. As it was slow on many that followed. My students and I tramped around the village all through the monsoon and through the month of Ashar, when people eat lush leafy greens such as *kalmi, puishak,* or *kachu shak,* a sort of long as-paragus which acquires a delicate flavor and texture when boiled. My favorite smell came from the delicious *kachu shak* as it sim-mered with bay leaves, ground cumin, and turmeric in the village.

Very early on in the process of trying to convince women to be-come Grameen Bank borrowers, we realized that having female bank workers made the job a great deal easier. The process of breaking down fear was always my greatest challenge and it was made easier by the careful work and gentle voices of my female workers. Still, results were slow in coming. At the end of every day, I would debrief my students. Often women workers would come with the names of potential borrowers jotted down on the back of cigarette packs. As a result, I hired three young women to work in our pilot project—Nurjahan Begum and Jannat Quanine, two recent graduates of the university, and Priti Rani Barua, who lived in the Buddhist section of Jobra and had only a ninth-grade education. These female workers found it easier to establish a rapport with women in the villages than their male counterparts, but they also faced many obstacles. Indeed, our fight against the ill treatment and segregation of women took place not only on behalf of our borrowers but also on behalf of our own female employees.

The nature of a bank worker's job requires that he or she walk alone in rural areas, sometimes for distances as long as five miles in each direction. The parents of many prospective female bank workers found this demeaning—even scandalous. Though they might have allowed their daughter to sit behind an office desk, they did not accept her spending her day working in the villages for Grameen. How could the female bank workers get from place to place? Men can ride bicycles in Bangladesh, but it is often considered improper for women to do so. We bought training bikes and held classes to make our women workers confident bike riders. But in some places, the locals would attack them for riding bicycles. Though the villagers would permit women to ride in bullock carts, baby taxis, rickshaws, or even motorbikes, the religious conservatives could not accept a woman on a bike. Even today, twenty-five years later, when 94 percent of our borrowers are women, our female employees still face hostility and discrimination on a regular basis in the villages where they work. When a female bank worker visits a village for the first time, it is not uncommon for crowds to gather and observe her. She often faces criticism from the villagers who were not used to seeing women anywhere but in the home.

We usually tried to recruit our women workers when they had just finished their studies and were either waiting to be married or were married with an unemployed husband. Generally, for an unmarried woman, being employed immediately removed some of the family pressure to get married. In addition, having a job increases her marriage prospects dramatically. She is no longer seen as a burden.

Retaining female bank workers has proven very difficult. Typically, if a female Grameen bank worker gets married, her in-laws exert pressure on her to quit her job. They do not want a "decent" young woman walking alone around villages. They also worry that she might not be able to defend herself in case of trouble. After her first child, the pressure grows for the female bank worker to quit her job. And then after the second or third child, the woman often wants to spend more time at home with her children. And the miles of walking that she did as a young woman are not as easy for her. When we announced our pension program in 1994, which included an early retirement option, we were saddened though not too surprised that many of our female employees opted to leave Grameen. Often we are criticized in international conferences for not employing enough women. I believe that most of those who attack us do not understand the social reality of Bangladesh, but I admit that their criticisms have encouraged us to redouble our efforts and devise new ways to retain female employees. In fact, in 1997 we celebrated the promotion of one woman to the position of zonal manager, the most senior field-based position in Grameen. But the loss of many rank-and-file female employees through retirement since 1994 has been disheartening.

The story of Nurjahan illustrates many of the pressures on our young female workers. Nurjahan was a graduate student at Chittagong University when we started our Grameen experiment. She was twenty-three and studying to get her master's degree with honors in Bengali literature. She had lost her father when she was eleven. She came from a conservative middle-class family and her mother wanted her to marry and have children. But after she completed her studies, Nurjahan rebelled. She was the first woman in her village to receive a master's degree, and she was proud of a job offer she received from a nongovernmental organization (NGO). She begged her mother to allow her to work. But her mother refused, arguing that girls of good families in Bangladesh are not supposed to work at all. Nurjahan's brother was willing to let her work for the NGO, but he was concerned about what others in the village would say. So Nurjahan kept delaying her starting date. The NGO postponed the date three times, but finally could not wait any longer, and she lost the job offer.

When Grameen offered Nurjahan a job, her mother and brothers finally relented. Nurjahan did not tell them that she would have no office and no desk and that she would spend her days walking through the poorest areas of the poorest villages, talking to beggars and destitute women. She knew they would be horrified and would force her to quit. She began working with us in October 1977. And for as long as her family did not know what Grameen was like, they grudgingly allowed her to work.

On her first day, I asked Nurjahan to do a case study of Ammajan Amina, a poor woman of Jobra village who had no means of subsistence. I did this for three reasons. First, I believe that the best way to inspire a new worker is to let her see firsthand the real-life problems of the poor. I wanted Nurjahan to have her heart touched by the reality of poverty. Second, I wanted to see how Nurjahan would cope. It is not easy to work with the poor and to do so in a way that will positively affect their lives. Nurjahan's master's degree did not ensure that she possessed the inner motivation, confidence, and strength to show these people how to overcome obstacles. Would she be willing to spend time with the destitute? To learn how they live, work, and survive? She had to learn to view her clients as total human beings in need of help and change. She had to establish an easy and fear-free interaction with the poor and find out everything there was to know about her borrowers' lives and difficulties. Thus, on Nurjahan's first day, I pulled her aside and said, "Try to speak with Ammajan Amina alone. Try to touch her and to understand her mentality. Today, go there with no pen and no paper in order to gain her confidence."

Nurjahan went to Jobra with my colleague Assaduzzaman ("Assad" for short). Nodding toward Assad, Ammajan Amina asked Nurjahan, "Is he your husband?"

"No," Nurjahan answered, "he is just a colleague."

"Why are you coming to see us with a man who is not your husband?" asked Ammajan Amina. This seemed to be in conflict with the practice of *purdah* and made her suspicious of Nurjahan.

But little by little, day after day, Nurjahan won over Amina's confidence. Amina shared her past with Nurjahan. Of Amina's six children, four had died of hunger or disease. Only two daughters survived. Her husband, much older than she, was quite ill. For several years, he had spent most of the family assets on medicines. After his death, all that Amina had left was the house. She was in her forties, old by Bangladesh standards where, contrary to the world norm, women have a lower life expectancy than men. She was illiterate and had never earned an income before. She tried selling homemade cakes and cookies door to door without much success. Her in-laws tried to expel her and the children from the house where she had lived for twenty years, but she refused to leave.

One day Amina returned and found her brother-in-law had sold her tin roof, and the buyer was now busy removing it. Now the rainy season started, and Amina was cold, hungry, and too poor to make food to sell. As she had no roof to protect her house, the monsoon destroyed her mud walls. She used all she had to feed her own children. Because she was a proud woman, she only begged in nearby villages. One day when she returned she found her house had collapsed, and she started screaming, "Where is my daughter? Where is my baby?"

She found her older child dead under the rubble of her house.

When Nurjahan first met with her in 1976, Ammajan Amina held her only surviving child in her arms. She was heartbroken and desperate. There was no question of any moneylender, much less a commercial bank, giving her credit. But with Grameen loans she bought bamboo to make baskets. Amina remained a borrower to the end of her days. Now her daughter is a member of Grameen.

Through her experience with Amina and many such fragile cases, it became clear to me that Nurjahan had a special gift for dealing with the poor. I was very pleased to have her on my team of workers. Then one day Nurjahan's sister-in-law's brother came to give Nurjahan some family news. When he arrived at our office, he saw that it was only a tin-roofed shack with no telephone, toilet, or running water. He was shocked. This was not at all the image he had of a commercial bank. The office manager, Assad, told Nurjahan's in-law that she was out in the field. The man went and found Nurjahan seated on the grass under a tree talking to some village women. He was astonished. Nurjahan was so embarrassed that she lied and told him that that day was a special situation and begged him not to tell her mother what he had seen. But he did.

At first, Nurjahan's mother was furious. Like most conservative Bengali Muslims, she felt that her daughter should hide indoors, observing the custom of *purdah*. She could not imagine Nurjahan working under the open sky or that such work was decent and becoming to a respectable woman. But eventually, once Nurjahan told her mother the truth and explained her deep desire to help the poor, her mother relented. Today, she is a big supporter of Grameen.

One day I asked Nurjahan to make a presentation about Grameen at a cultural festival. She was to travel to the town of Comilla with two junior female bank workers, and because the trip from Chittagong to Comilla is not dangerous, I did not make any provision for a male colleague to accompany them. This was not insensitive on my part. I felt that my workers ought to fend for themselves. Also, I knew that Grameen needed to break the myth that a woman could not travel alone on a short trip.

Though she did not show it, Nurjahan was furious with me for not placing her in the care of a man who would arrange the travel plans and take care of all the details of the road. She even telephoned a male colleague and asked him to accompany her, but he was busy. As she had never traveled alone before, she prayed to Allah to give her strength and courage, and away she went. The show in Comilla was a great success.

Now Nurjahan travels everywhere she pleases without difficulty. She is one of the three general managers of the Grameen Bank and heads our training division, where she helps hundreds of our future young bank workers to become self-reliant.

CHAPTER

SIX

Expanding Beyond

Jobra into Tangail

In the fall of 1977, on the first anniversary of our rural banking experiment, I joined my family in Chittagong for the holy festival of Eid-ul Fitr, which celebrates the end of the monthlong fast of Ramadan. Though Eid-ul Fitr is a three-day holiday, like most Bengali families we take a week to celebrate it. My mother and father, both extremely religious, instilled a deep respect for tradition in their children. My father spends the entire Ramadan paying the religious tax (*Jakat*) required by the Quran. As prescribed by Shariah law, he gives first to family relatives who are in need, then to poor neighbors, and finally to the poor at large.

Eid-ul Fitr is our opportunity to gather together relatives and reflect on the year that has elapsed. In 1977, we congregated at Niribili, the house my father built in 1959 in the then-new Pachlaish residential area of Chittagong. *Niribili* means peace and quiet. The house rises behind a protective garden wall, surrounded by a ring of lush green trees: mango, betel nut, banana, teak, guava, coconut, and grenadine. Niribili is huge. With its vast verandahs and wide-open spaces, I have always felt that it resembles a transatlantic steamer. Despite its constructional oddities—the rooms are too big, the hallways too lavish and impractical—I love the place. It is divided into eight separate apartments, which house my brothers, so that my father, who lives on the ground floor, is surrounded by half of his large, loving brew. That is the way he likes it. The house is a source of family strength and unity.

On the day of Eid, our family's ritual is fixed according to custom. We rise early and wash. Then we visit Batua, my father's ancestral village, where I was born and where the family spent most of the Second World War. At 7 A.M. the men of the family head for the Eidgah, an open field where a large congregation gathers for prayer. We say our *namaz* (prayer) and the imam begins his *Khutbah* (sermon). Several thousand people line up behind him. Everyone is dressed in new Eid clothes and the smell of traditional perfumes fills the open field. After prayer my brothers and I embrace each other, saying, "Eid Mubarak" ("Happy Eid") and line up to touch Father's feet as a mark of respect and greeting. After a visit to the cemetery and the payment of the compulsory *fitra* tax (1.25 kilos of wheat to the poor), we begin our round of visits to relatives' houses. After our monthlong fast, the sweetmeats and delicious noodle dishes taste all the better.

Mumtaz, our elder sister, prepares the best sweets of all. This year she has made my favorites: creamy *rashomalai,* with tiny white poppy seeds and a rich mango pulp mixed into *kheer,* a sort of thick evaporated milk. I savor her yogurt and *chira,* delicious rice flakes, complemented by sweet mangoes and bananas.

Mumtaz is twelve years older than I. She has an oval face with warm dark eyes. Though she married and left the house at seventeen, she always made it her business to oversee her siblings as if she were a substitute mother. This Eid-ul Fitr of 1977, children were all around us, calling out to each other, laughing, eating, and playing. But Mumtaz quietly took my hands in hers. How good she is! How caring and loving she has been to me, to all of us! As I look into her eyes, I recall the day in 1950 when I raced by bus and rickshaw all the way to her house to announce the birth of my brother Ayub. How out of breath I was, how excited at ten. She laughed and embraced me and called her neighbors to tell them the good news. We ate and celebrated long into the night, and the next day Mumtaz packed her bag and moved into our house to help Mother take care of little Ayub. So much time had passed since then. Looking around the room at my sisters Mumtaz and Tunu and my brothers Salam, Ibrahim, Jahangir, Ayub, Azam, and Moinu, I thanked God for our health and happiness. How lucky we were.

■

In October 1977, on a trip to the capital city of Dhaka, I had a chance meeting that radically changed our efforts to bring credit to the poor villagers of Jobra. For personal reasons that had nothing to do with Grameen, I was in the offices of one of our largest national banks, the Bangladesh Krishi ("Agriculture") Bank (BKB), where I bumped into an acquaintance of mine, the managing director. As soon as he saw me, Mr. A. M. Anisuzzaman, an extremely talkative and outgoing man, launched into a tirade, a long monologue attacking me and other academics who were not doing enough for Bangladesh but hiding away in our ivory towers. It was a blistering attack:

"You academics are failing us. You are failing in your social duties. And the banking system of this country stinks. It is all corruption and embezzlement and filth. Millions of taka are stolen every year from the BKB bank without any trace. No one is accountable to anyone for anything. Certainly not you lily-white–handed academics with your cushy jobs and your jaunts abroad. You are useless all of you. Utterly useless! I am absolutely disgusted by what I see in this society. No one thinks of the poor. I tell you this country is a disgrace, and it deserves all the problems it has."

Anisuzzaman went on and on. When at last he began to slow down, I said, "Well, sir, I am happy to hear you say all this because I just happen to have a proposal that may interest you."

I proceeded to outline my Jobra experiment, explaining that my students were volunteering on an unsalaried basis. "They donate their time and I use the budget for my practical training to pay for expenses. The loans are being repaid and the situation of our borrowers is improving by the day. But I do worry about my students. They need to be compensated, even in a small way, for doing this work. The entire experiment is held together only by a thread. It needs institutional support."

Anisuzzaman listened carefully to my story. As I spoke, I saw him drawn to my idea. He was getting excited.

"What problems have you had with the Janata Bank?" he asked.

"They insist that I guarantee each and every loan. I will be in America for three months, attending UN General Assembly sessions, and they will insist on mailing the loan documents for me to sign. You can imagine how impractical that is!"

He shook his head. "Tell me what I can do to help you."

I was delighted. I could have gone on for years and years and never have run across such an eager supporter. I explained, "The Janata Bank can't raise objections to our program because there has been no loan default. But it takes them anywhere from two to six months to process each new loan. Every single one has to be sanctioned by the head office in Dhaka. And every time they have a question, it takes a few more months to go up the chain of command and come back again. It is difficult to operate like this."

Anisuzzaman waved his hand impatiently. "You can't go on like this. It is absurd. Now tell me what you would want from me?"

"From the Krishi Bank?"

"Yes."

"Well." My mind was racing. "I guess I would like the Agriculture Bank to set up a branch in Jobra and leave it at my disposal. I would frame its rules and procedures and recruit my own staff. And you would allow me to grant loans up to a total of 1 million taka. Give me a 1 million taka limit, give me one year, then close the lid and let me go to work. A year later, open the lid and see if I am still alive. If you like just one thing I have done, extend the program. If not, simply close down the branch and forget about it. Use me as an experiment. If no one repays any of our loans, then at most you have lost 1 million taka."

"Fine," said Anisuzzaman. He picked up the telephone and said to his secretary, "Get me the manager of the Chittagong District. He covered the receiver and asked, "When are you going back to Chittagong?"

"Tomorrow."

"By the afternoon plane?"

"Yes."

Another voice sounded on the line and Anisuzzaman said, "My friend, Professor Yunus, is flying back from Dhaka tomorrow. He will arrive at the university campus at 5 P.M. I want you to be waiting for him at his residence, and I want you to take orders from him. Whatever he says, whatever he wants, those are orders from me. Do you understand?"

"Yes, sir."

"Have you any questions?" Anisuzzaman said into the telephone.

"No, sir."

"Perfect. Now I don't want to hear anything going wrong. I don't want Professor Yunus complaining to my office that his orders are not being followed. Do you understand?"

As I came out of Anisuzzaman's office, my head still swimming, I saw a girl sweeping the street outside. She was extremely thin, barefoot, and wore a ring in her nose. Like the thousands of cleaners in Dhaka's streets, this woman would work all day long, seven days a week, and would just barely earn enough to subsist. Yet she was one of the "lucky ones," for she had a job. It was for this very woman, and for all those women who could not even aspire to a job of street cleaner, that I wanted to develop my credit

program. At that moment, I knew that I was doing the right
thing.

■

The next afternoon, the Chittagong regional manager of the
Agriculture Bank, was waiting for me in my drawing room. He
seemed very nervous. I told him what had happened the day before and how enthusiastically Anisuzzaman had embraced the
work my students and I were doing in Jobra. The manager explained that I would need to write a project proposal. He would
bring several of his colleagues to my house to draft a formal written request for funding.

The following Monday, five people showed up at my home.
They asked me a million questions, things I had never thought
about: How many borrowers did I want? How many employees?
What salary levels would I offer? How many safes would I need? I
answered the questions the best I could. A few weeks later I received a large envelope in the mail. It was a proposal based on
what I had told them I wanted to do, a long complicated thick
tome, full of bureaucratic jargon. Even reading a single page was
extremely difficult. It said nothing. I took out a pen and jotted
down my original idea in my own words. My proposal was to the
point. The first thing I changed was the name of the branch. I
wrote:

Krishi Bank uses the term "agriculture" in its title. I do not
want this branch to be about agriculture. Farmers are not the
poorest people in Bangladesh. On the contrary, those who
own farms are relatively well off compared to the destitute
landless who make a living by selling labor. I want this branch
to cover all sorts of rural employment, such as trading, small
manufacturing, retailing, even selling door to door. I want this

to be a rural bank, not a bank merely concerned with crops and farms. So I choose the word "Grameen."*

Several months went by before I heard from Anisuzzaman. He called me in for a meeting in his office in Dhaka. Once I had seated myself, he lit a cigarette and considered me carefully.

"My board of directors say that I have no authority to do what I am trying to do," he said. "I can't delegate my banking authority to you because you are an outsider, not an employee of the bank." Anisuzzaman paused to frame his question. "Yunus, do you really want to open a new branch of our bank?"

"No, not at all. I just want to lend money to the poor," I answered.

"Do you want to remain a professor?"

"Well, teaching is the only thing I know how to do. It's what I love."

"I am not pressuring you. I was only thinking out loud." Anisuzzaman leaned his head back and blew smoke up to the ceiling. "You could give up your job at the university and simply become an employee of our bank. That would make it easy for me to make you my deputy. I could then delegate any of my powers to you without fear of complaints from the board."

"Thank you, but I have no real interest in becoming a banker," I answered. "I would rather remain a professor. I have a department to run, students and professors to oversee, university politics to contend with. I am doing this poverty alleviation work with my left hand, as it were. I would far rather name one of my students to be the manager of the branch."

Anisuzzaman stared out the window of his office, letting the smoke curl from his cigarette. I could see his mind toying with var-

---

*Grameen derives from the word *gram,* or "village." Its adjectival form *grameen* means "rural," or "of the village."

ious ideas. "What if I do not make you responsible for the branch on paper. Officially, the district manager would oversee the branch, but unofficially he would do everything you tell him. He would take his orders from you. And if there were anything out of the ordinary, he would come to headquarters, and I would approve it. You should submit a list of your students who are currently working for you in Jobra. One of them can become the branch manager and the others can become regular employees of the bank."

I smiled at the thought that my associates—Assad, Nurjahan, and Jannat—would finally have solid, paying jobs for the first time in their lives. "I would call it the Grameen Branch," I said.

Anisuzzaman nodded, "The Experimental Grameen Branch of the Agriculture Bank. How does that sound?"

"Perfect."

We were both smiling now. He got up. We stood by the window. Outside, the chaos of the city streamed by. I saw barefoot beggars with babies, women asleep on the sidewalk, children with deformed limbs and emaciated bodies.

"The urban poor are another problem," Anisuzzaman said with a loud sigh.

"If we alleviate suffering in the countryside, that will reduce the pressure on the poor to rush to Dhaka and clog the streets," I said.

He nodded slowly. "Good luck, Professor."

■

I immediately threw myself into my work. Still a full-time professor at the university, I devoted much of my day to managing our Jobra branch of the Agriculture Bank, which was still staffed by my ex-students. We could work faster than with the Janata Bank, and I no longer needed to guarantee each loan personally, but we still had fewer than five hundred borrowers. Though there were many individual successes, we did not seem to be making much of a dent in the chronic poverty of the villages.

After a few months, in early 1978, I was invited to preside over a session at a seminar called "Financing the Rural Poor" organized by the Central Bank. The seminar was under the aegis of the United States Agency for International Development (USAID) and attended by a group of experts from Ohio State University. These U.S. experts argued that the key to lending to farmers was setting interest rates at a high level. They believed that when threatened with higher interest farmers would repay more consistently.

This made no sense to me. I protested: "When farmers in Bangladesh are desperate, they will borrow regardless of what interest they are charged. They will even go to a moneylender who threatens to take over all their possessions." The men in the conference room looked at me uneasily. "I would pay farmers a negative interest rate," I explained. "I would lend them one hundred taka (about five dollars), and if a farmer returned ninety to me, then I would forgive him the repayment of the ten taka. You see, the real problem with lending to farmers is getting the principal back, not the interest."

I was being intentionally provocative. These policy experts wanted to make credit so difficult that only skilled farmers and artisans would dare to borrow money. I, on the other hand, wanted to make it easier for people so that they would be encouraged to pay back their loans.

One elderly banker had little patience for my lecture. "Professor Yunus," he began, "your Jobra experiment is nothing, only a flyspeck compared to the big national banks we manage. Our hair has not turned gray for nothing. We have a lot of experience. If you want to prove your point, show us success over a whole district, not just in a single village."

I was not surprised by his challenge. Most bankers did not take me seriously. They glossed over my desire to extend the program and remained entrenched in their belief that it was unworkable on a national level.

The deputy governor of the Central Bank, Mr. Asit Kumar Gangopadhaya, was in the audience listening to this whole discussion. After the meeting, he called me into his office and asked me if I was serious about wanting to extend my experiment. I told him I was. A month later he invited me to a meeting of all the managing directors of the state-owned banks to discuss my proposal.

The directors received me with indulgent and patronizing attitudes. When Gangopadhaya asked them for their support they said, "Of course, no problem at all," but it was clearly lip service to please him. In truth, they had deep reservations. They argued that borrowers were repaying their loans simply because I was a highly respected university professor and that micro-credit worked in Chittagong because I was a native of that city. I tried to explain that the poor did not go to my university, that none of their families could read and write, and that my academic reputation was meaningless to them, but the directors around the table were not listening. If I was serious about demonstrating that this project was replicable by any other bank, I would resign my professorship, become a banker, and set up a Grameen branch in another district.

■

In the end, I did just that. The University of Chittagong granted me a two-year leave of absence. On June 6, 1979, before I knew what had happened, I had officially joined the Grameen Bank Project in the District of Tangail.

Tangail was selected because it was close to Dhaka and it would be easy for them to judge if the program was having any real impact on the villagers. It was agreed that each national bank would make three branches available to us—one small bank offered only one branch—giving us a total of nineteen branches in Tangail, six branches in Chittagong, and the Agriculture Bank branch we had already created in Jobra. Suddenly, Grameen was twenty-five bank branches strong.

Tangail District was in the throes of a warlike situation. Armed gangs in an underground Marxist dissident movement called the Gonobahini ("The People's Army") terrorized the countryside. These guerrillas killed with little compunction. They simply pointed a gun and fired. In every village we came across dead bodies lying in the middle of the road, hanging from trees, or shot by a wall. The countryside was awash with arms and ammunition left over from the War of Liberation. To save their lives, most of the local community leaders had run away, hidden with neighbors, or moved into hotels in Tangail City. There was neither law nor order.

What could we, a fledgling bank project, achieve in the face of this bloodshed and killing? We worried about the physical safety of our newly recruited branch managers and bank workers who would bê working and living by themselves in distant villages. To make matters worse, many of the young workers we were hiring were ex-students with radical sympathies, who could easily be swayed by the armed leftist guerrillas. (In fact, we later found out that some of our workers had been active Gonobahini members up until they began working for us.)

It was the hottest part of the year. Even the slightest effort left one completely exhausted. During the day the roads were deserted and people stood under trees praying for a *kalbaisakhi,* a sudden summer storm. The villages we passed through seemed so godforsaken and the people so poor and emaciated that I knew I had come to the right place. This is where we were needed most.

The staff at the banks through which we were supposed to operate resented us for adding to their workload. Countless times they refused to provide services or actively opposed us. Once the situation got so bad that one of our own officers aimed his gun at the manager of a local commercial bank and threatened to kill the man on the spot if he did not make more funds available to Grameen borrowers. We had to fire the officer. The assaulted manager asked to be sent back to Dhaka, and it soured relations with that bank.

We did not give up. Rather than depend on the unreliable staff at the national banks, we tried to do as much of our own work as possible. The ex-Gonobahini turned out to be excellent workers. These underground fighters were young (usually between eighteen and twenty years old), hard working, and dedicated. They had wanted to liberate the country with guns and revolution, and now they were walking around those same villages extending micro-loans to the destitute. They just needed a cause to fight for. We channeled their energies toward something more constructive than terrorism. Provided they gave up their guns, we were happy to hire them as bank workers.

At first I just had a skeleton staff that came up from Jobra with me: my young associates Assad, Dipal, and Sheikh Abdud Daiyan. Then later, when it was judged safe, I brought two of the female colleagues who had also worked in Jobra: Nurjahan and Jannat. I moved into a building that was still under construction. I lived in a tiny unfinished room on the third floor with laborers working all around me. During Ramadan I broke the daily fast with the traditional light meal of *iftar* in the evening: pressed rice, called *chira,* sweetened with ground coconut and sugar, chickpeas fried with red chilies, slices of mango, and flat disks of fried ground lentils seasoned with green chili and onion.

I had no toilet in my office. When I wanted to relieve myself during the day, I had to disturb my neighbors. What kept my spirits up in those first difficult days was the startling generosity of the locals. At night an old neighbor living under a badly thatched roof would often offer me some *pantabhat,* leftover rice soaked in water, fermented, and seasoned with hot fried chilies, raw onions, and leftover vegetables. Unfortunately, Grameen had made it a rule not to accept food or gifts from any borrower or villager. Reluctantly, I refused his offer.

Every tiny decision I made had to be reviewed by all the managing directors of all the participating banks at the regular monthly meeting of the Central Bank of Bangladesh in Dhaka. This was a slow and ponderous process. For example, we wasted two hours on Decision Number 37, arguing back and forth about whether to give flashlights to bank workers so they could walk between villages at night. One managing director felt that village life in Bangladesh ought not to be "ruined" by the importation of flashlights. He wanted our bank workers to use old-fashioned lanterns and kerosene lamps. Like the social anthropologists who continually accuse Grameen of fundamentally altering rural society in Bangladesh, this banker was not willing to allow the introduction of anything that sounded nontraditional. With wealth comes change. But why is this a drawback? I am all for change. And if that managing director lived in the poorest villages of Tangail and Chittagong, he would be all for it too.

In March 1980, I was remarried in a big ceremony in Dhaka. My marriage to Vera had come to an end several years before. Soon after the birth of our daughter Monica in March 1977, Vera determined to leave Bangladesh, saying that it was not a good place to raise a child. Though we still loved each other, we simply could not agree to settle in the same place. Vera refused to stay and I could not abandon Bangladesh. With great sadness, we agreed on a divorce in December. Unlike Vera, who came from a culture so foreign to my own, Afrozi Begum was a Bangladeshi researcher in advanced physics at the University of Manchester. She was as comfortable in the eastern and western worlds as I was. For a few months after our wedding, Afrozi remained in England to finish her research while I worked in Tangail. But soon she joined me in Tangail, where we lived on the third floor of our office buildings. Since then, we have always lived close to our office, and even today we live within the office complex. The only difference now is that we have our daughter Deena Afroz Yunus, who was born on January 24, 1986.

By November 1982, Grameen Bank membership had grown to 28,000, of which fewer than half were women. How did we achieve this jump from the 500 Jobra members we had in 1979? There was no one secret to the success of our Tangail expansion, but surely the hard work and dedication of our bank workers and managers was an essential part of it. From those early days, we learned the importance of picking fresh young people to run our branches. Surprisingly, people without previous work experience of any kind are often best suited for this. Previous work experience distracts new workers from the ideals and unique procedures of Grameen.

Many young managers embraced Grameen as a great opportunity. They loved the thrill of experiment and adventure. Responsible for setting up the local Grameen branch, the manager chooses the general location of the future office and draws a map of the area. He writes reports on the village's history, culture, economy, and poverty situation. To give Grameen maximum exposure, the manager then invites all the people in nearby villages, including village leaders, religious leaders, teachers, and government officials, to a "projection meeting" at which a high-ranking Grameen official explains the bank's procedures in detail, giving the villagers the option to either accept Grameen with all its rules and regulations or to reject it, in which case the bank promises to leave the area. So far, no one has ever asked us to leave, but we like to make it clear from the start that the choice to have us is theirs.

Working in a bank for the poor is highly specialized work. This is true from the planning and designing level on down to the person-to-person contact in the field. Visitors to Grameen often ask me, "What makes a Grameen worker or manager so different from other young people? Why are they so willing to work under such harsh conditions?" I believe the answer, in large part, is the training program for bank employees that emerged from the informal weekly review meetings I used to have with our staff in Tangail in the early 1980s. When most people talk about training in the context of an antipoverty program, they mean teaching poor people new skills. In Grameen, we offer our borrowers little if any formal training. Instead, we train our staff, turning them into an elite brigade of poverty fighters.

Anyone younger than twenty-eight with a master's degree and at least a B average in all final examinations is eligible to apply for a job as one of our bank managers. We advertise in the national newspapers and receive a large number of applications. Half of these applicants would make first-class bank managers for Grameen. But since our training facilities are limited, we screen the candidates through interviews to pick only a limited number. Those we select are asked to report to our training institute. Here they receive a two-day briefing, and then we send them off to various branches, where they remain in training for most of the following six months. Before they go, the institute staff tells them, "Observe everything carefully. When your training is over, your task will be to create a Grameen branch of your own that will be better in every respect than the one in which you spent your first six months."

So trainees discover Grameen for themselves by watching others run one of our branches. We immerse each new young worker in the Grameen culture and the culture of the poor, teaching him or her to appreciate the unexplored potential of the destitute. Our staff training is simple, but tough and rigorous. The bulk of it is self-taught. There are no reading materials to go through or computer programs to learn. We find that the villages of Bangladesh teach young people more about life than the pages of any book ever could. During this time we encourage them to criticize everything they see and come up with proposals for modifications or improvements to any procedures. When they reassemble at our training institute in the Dhaka headquarters, they present their improvement proposals to their colleagues. After their spell in the field, the trainees always bring in a breath of fresh air. They also bring keen observations and sharp criticisms. Often they report that our sacred rules are violated or that our clockwork precision is crumbling down. They come with major plans for overhauling our operations and terrible punishments for those who violate our rules. In the ensuing open debate, the sharpness of these criticisms often gets blunted, but still there are elements of truth in what they report. We encourage these spirited debates, for innovation can only sprout in an atmosphere of tolerance, diversity, and curiosity.

Unlike our managers, our bank workers do not have master's degrees. They have only two years of college education. If they were to enter the government, they might become junior clerks or office helpers, and they would be at the bottom of the office hierarchy. We receive thousands of applications each year for bank worker positions, but unfortunately we can only accept about one in ten applicants.

We make an effort to hire trainees from a wide variety of economic backgrounds. The overwhelming majority of our job applicants (85 percent for men, 97 percent for women) who come to interview with us have never visited Dhaka before. To raise the money necessary to pay for their interview trip, their parents often sell crops, standing trees, cows, goats, or ornaments. The parents of at least half of our applicants borrow money to finance the trip, many from moneylenders. Over half of our candidates arrive in Dhaka on the same day as their interview as they do not have friends or relatives to spend the night with and they cannot afford a hotel or a guest house.

Nearly all our applicants are good persons imbued with a strong sense of traditional values. Most of them pray five times a day, as expected of a Muslim. The bank is hard work, but those we select appreciate the security, respectability, self-confidence, and opportunity it affords them. Their career prospects after working at Grameen are excellent. Though we pay the salary of an entry-level government worker, we find that privately owned commercial banks that offer much higher wages can rarely entice our workers away from us. What makes our staff so committed? Is it the work itself? Their training? The friendships they form? The sense of personal challenge, self-worth, and rectitude they get from helping their country? I suppose that every worker has his or her own reasons. In any case, we encourage our workers to be politically and socially aware. And we trust them to analyze the objective reality and come up with their own conclusions. Above all, we want to build a problem-solving attitude among our workers. We firmly believe that every problem has multiple solutions and that it is our job to select the best one.

Unlike other commercial bank workers, our staff members grow to consider themselves teachers. They are teachers in the sense that they help their borrowers to explore their full potential, to discover their strengths, to extend their capabilities further than ever before. I, too, consider myself a teacher. Many of the senior officials at Grameen were my students at Chittagong University, and I am happy that they consider me more as a teacher than as a boss. With a boss, one has to be formal, but with a teacher the relationship is more informal, even spiritual. One can discuss one's problems and weaknesses more freely. One can admit personal mistakes without fear of triggering an official sanction. Traditional bank officials need their office, their papers, their desk, and their telephone for support. They feel lost without these props. But you can strip everything away from a Grameen employee, and still at heart he or she remains a teacher.

■

Here is a typical Grameen bank worker, a composite of the 12,000 workers we now employ, and a typical day's work:

1. Name: Akhtar Hossain

2. Age: 27

3. Monthly salary (1995): 2,200 taka ($66), including housing allowance, medical subsidy, and commuting allowance

4. Bonus: One month's salary paid during each of the two Eid holidays

- 6 A.M. Akhtar wakes up, washes, prays, eats breakfast.

- 7 A.M. Akhtar fetches his bicycle, documents, and carrying bag from the branch and pedals to a center.

- 7:30 A.M. Forty bank borrowers await Akhtar at the center. They are seated in eight rows, organized according to group. Each group chairperson holds the passbooks of the five group members. Akhtar collects the loan repayments and deposits from each group.

- 9:30 A.M. Akhtar bicycles to another center for his second meeting. During the course of the week, he attends to ten different centers, meeting with all 400 borrowers he is responsible for and collecting repayments for general loans, seasonal loans, and housing loans, as well as savings deposits.

- 11 A.M. Akhtar visits borrowers at home and offers advice. This is an important way to keep track of his borrowers' needs and problems.

- Noon. Back at the branch office, Akhtar fills out all the reporting forms and enters all the records in his ledger. The branch manager signs off.

- 1:30–2:00 P.M. Akhtar takes a lunch break with his fellow workers.

- 2 P.M. Funds collected in the morning are disbursed as new loans in the afternoon. All workers help the branch manager with this task.

- 3 P.M. Once the loan disbursements are finished, Akhtar and his fellow workers record the new loan information in the ledgers.

- 4:30 P.M. Akhtar takes a tea break and chats with his fellow workers.

- 5:00–6:30 P.M. Akhtar visits a center that is experiencing difficulties with loans or organizes an educational outreach program for local children.

- 7:00 P.M. Akhtar returns to the office, finishes some paperwork, and retires for the day.

During our Tangail expansion, we also developed a procedure for establishing new bank branches. Whenever Grameen opened a branch in a new location, we made a great effort to work slowly and deliberately. No branch would try to reach more than a hundred borrowers in its first year of operation. Only once a branch successfully received the full repayment of its first one hundred loans was it allowed to speed up operations and recruit more borrowers. Our goal was to liberate the potential of the poor to create better lives for themselves, not to force individuals to do anything they do not want to. Why hurry? Grameen's objective was to develop a system that worked, not to rush out a service that would fail its borrowers. Therefore we started small. The manager, usually accompanied by an associate manager who will eventually take over responsibility for setting up his or her own new branch, arrives in an area where Grameen has decided to establish a branch. They arrive without any formal introduction. They have no office, no place to stay, and no one to get in touch with. Their first assignment is to document everything about the area.

Why do we provide them with so little orientation? We want them to appear as different as possible from the usual government officials who arrive in the villages with great pomp, expecting delicious meals and comfortable accommodations at the rich villagers' houses. Grameen tries to create a new breed of "officials" with fresh ideas and modest ways. Therefore our managers and associates must pay for a room and are not permitted to stay in fancy surroundings. They may find shelter at some abandoned house, school hostel, or local council office. They must decline offers of food from the well-to-do, explaining that this is against Grameen rules.

Every day, the new branch manager and associate manager walk for miles to meet with villagers and explain the procedures for forming credit groups and our policy of accepting only the most disadvantaged—women who are located the farthest away from the proposed location of the branch. Come rain or shine, they never stop visiting the poor. They are not allowed to take shortcuts by appointing villagers as agents, the usual practice of government officials. And ultimately, it is not their words but their hard work that softens the attitude of the villagers.

Still, it can be a battle. Often the villagers do not believe these modest visitors are bank officials at all. The local schoolteachers are usually the first ones to recognize the visitors' educational status. But none of these teachers have ever made it to university, and they find it hard to believe that anyone with a master's degree would ever work in such a miserable village with such poor people, walking several miles every day. Often new managers face skepticism from religious and political leaders in the villages. It was in Tangail that we first encountered large-scale opposition from conservative clerics. In numerous cases these figures tried to scare uneducated villagers by telling them that a woman who takes loans from Grameen is trespassing into an evil area, forbidden to women. They warn her that as punishment for joining Grameen, she will not be given a proper Islamic burial when she dies—a terrifying prospect for a woman who has nothing.

Other rumors, which can be as frightening to a poor woman as they seem ludicrous to Grameen staff, often surface in the villages. Maharani Das, age thirty-five, from the coastal region of Pathuakali, was told that contact with Grameen would turn her into a Christian. Her family beat her repeatedly to prevent her from joining. Musammat Kuti Begum, age twenty, from Faridpur, joined Grameen in spite of being warned that the bank would take her to the Middle East and sell her to a slave trader. Mosammat Manikjan Bibi, age thirty-five, from Paipara, said, "The moneylenders and the rich people told me that if I joined Grameen, I was a bad Muslim, and the bank would take me out to sea and drop me to the bottom of the ocean." Manzira Khatun, age thirty-eight, from the Rajshahi District, heard she would be tortured, have a number tattooed on her arm, and be sold into prostitution. Grameen was said to convert women to Christianity, to destroy Islam by taking women out of *purdah,* to steal houses and property, to kidnap women borrowers, to run away with any repaid loans, and to belong to an international smuggling ring or a new East India Company that would recolonize Bangladesh as the British had done two and a half centuries ago.

As soon as such rumors start—and the above list is by no means exhaustive—the situation can become tense very quickly. In one particular village in Tangail, for example, our Grameen manager was physically threatened by a religious leader. When the manager saw there was no way to reason with the mullah, he quietly closed the branch and left the village. He told potential members that his life had been threatened and that they would have to go through orientation meetings in the neighboring village. Some women made the daily trek to the neighboring village to form groups and join Grameen. But others, inspired by the way Grameen had bettered the lives of their neighbors in other villages, visited the religious leader and argued with him.

"Why did you threaten that Grameen manager?" they asked. "Grameen was coming here to our village to do nothing but good."

"Do you want to go to hell?" answered the mullah. "Grameen is a Christian organization! It wants to destroy the rules of *purdah*. That is why it has come."

"The Grameen manager is a Muslim, and he knows the Quran better than you! Besides, Grameen allows us to work at home, husking rice, weaving mats, or making bamboo stools, without ever going out. The bank comes to our house. How is that against *purdah*? The only one who is against *purdah* here is you, by making us travel miles to a neighboring village to get relief. You are the one who is destroying our lifestyle, not Grameen."

"Go to the moneylender, he is a good Muslim," answered the confused mullah.

"He charges 10 percent a week! If you don't want us to borrow from Grameen, then you lend us the money."

"Leave me alone. I have had enough of your harassing me day and night."

"It is you who harasses us by not letting Grameen come here," answered the women. "We will only go when you let Grameen into our village. We will come every day and harass you until you let the bank in."

"Oh, okay then, to hell with you all. If you want to damn yourselves to perdition forever, go ahead, join Grameen. I have tried my best to save you. No one can say I didn't try my best to warn you. So go, borrow, and be damned!"

The women were overjoyed. They rushed in a group to the neighboring village and told the Grameen manager that he could come back now that they had talked to the mullah and that he no longer had any objection. The manager thanked them for their persistence on his behalf but said that he would return only if the man who threatened him came and requested his return. He did not want any misunderstanding or any physical threats hanging over him and his Grameen colleagues.

And so the women returned to their village. Again they went and confronted their mullah. Again they argued with him, until he was so disgusted and tired of the whole matter he wished he had never gotten involved. Finally, at his wit's end, he agreed to invite the manager back into his village. It was not an extremely courteous invitation, but everyone heard it. That was the important part.

The women who are the most desperate, who have nothing to eat, who have been abandoned by their husbands and are trying to feed their children by begging, usually stand by their decision to join Grameen Bank no matter who threatens them. They have no other choice. In some cases they must either borrow from us or watch their children die. And those on the sidelines who watch but dare not ignore the terrible rumors about us soon find out that the Grameen managers' understanding of religious issues is often deeper than that of most of the people who accuse them of being anti-Muslim.

We believe that Islam is not at all a hindrance to the eradication of poverty through micro-credit programs. Islam does not inherently prevent women from making a living for themselves or from improving their economic situation. In 1994, the adviser on women's affairs to the president of Iran came to visit me in Dhaka, and when I asked her what she thought about Grameen, she said, "There is nothing in Shariah law or the Quran against what you are doing. Why should women be hungry and poor? On the contrary, what you are doing is terrific. You are helping to educate a whole generation of children. And thanks to Grameen loans, women can work at home, instead of sitting around."

Many Islamic scholars have also told us that the Shariah ban on the charging of interest cannot apply to Grameen, since the Grameen borrower is also an owner of the bank. The purpose of the religious injunction against interest is to protect the poor from usury, but where the poor own their own bank, the interest is in effect paid to the company they own, and therefore to themselves.

Still, it became a big challenge to train our bank workers to overcome opposition from political and religious leaders without endangering their safety and that of the women they were serving. We tried a variety of techniques, and after a few years we learned that our staff members should quietly go about their business in one tiny corner of the village. If just a handful of desperate women make a leap of faith and join Grameen, everything changes. They get their money, start to earn additional income, and nothing terrible happens to them. Others begin to show interest. We find that borrowing groups form quickly after the initial period of resistance. When the ice finally breaks, women who originally said no to us begin to say, "Why not? I need money, too. In fact, I need the money more desperately than those who already joined. And I can make better use of it!" Gradually people come to accept us, and opposition dies off. But in every new village, it is a battle to begin.

After all these struggles, repeated in thousands of villages, it is frustrating to hear people dismiss our accomplishments, arguing that Grameen's success is due to cultural factors that cannot be replicated elsewhere. To succeed in Bangladesh, in many ways we have had to struggle *against* our culture. In fact, we have had to create a counterculture that values women's economic contribution, rewards hard work, and punishes corrupt practices. Grameen actively discourages the practice of dowry payments and the overly rigid interpretations of *purdah*. Indeed, if one were to look for the country where it would be most difficult to have a program like Grameen Bank succeed, I think that Bangladesh would come to the top of the list. And when we see programs modeled on Grameen thriving in the Philippines, Malaysia, Vietnam, South Africa, and Bolivia, to name a few, it simply reminds us of the tremendous obstacles we have had to overcome in our own country with its a moribund economy, reactionary elites, and frequent natural disasters.

■

Toward the end of 1981, when our two-year experiment in Tangail was coming to an end, the Central Bank asked the managing directors of its member commercial banks to give an assessment of Grameen's work. I was puzzled by their reaction, for they chalked Grameen's success up to one factor—the devotion of myself and my staff. They were still convinced that the Grameen concept could not be expanded.

"Grameen is not really a bank," said one manager. "Grameen's staff does not sit in offices or keep bankers' hours. They work until midnight day after day and go door to door like Boy Scouts. This is not a model we could replicate. It depends too much on Professor Yunus's personality. We can't have a Yunus in every branch."

I was angry. Why should we be penalized for our hard work? Rather than admitting that Grameen had come up with a new banking structure, a new economic concept that could revolutionize the nature of banking, these executives kept trying to pin our success on the individual qualities of myself and my staff. This was the same reaction I had heard two years earlier when we were performing our experiment on a tiny scale in Jobra village.

But this quibble masked a greater concern. These commercial bankers preferred to lend large amounts of money to fewer clients. We, on the contrary, prided ourselves on our vast number of clients. Our annual report listed hundreds of microloans offered to a plethora of new businesses, everything from husking rice to making ice cream sticks, trading in brass, repairing radios, processing mustard oil, and cultivating jackfruit.

I looked around the table at these grave men. "Okay," I said, accepting their challenge. "Why don't you spread our experiment over a large, spread-out area. Choose the poorest, most remote places you can find. Make certain that they are so far apart that I could not possibly be in all those areas at once."

I pulled out a sheet of paper and with a pencil I drew up then and there a five-year expansion plan for the Grameen experiment. I also promised the Central Bank that it would not cost them a penny. I would mobilize the funds needed to execute the plan elsewhere.

■

Since my days at Chittagong University, one international organization had always come up with support when I asked for it. This was the Ford Foundation. Lincoln Chen, Stephen Biggs, and Bill Fuller, among others, have assisted us with our work. At this particular time, the foundation was especially interested in our experiment and eager to help us overcome the skepticism of the commercial bankers. Adrienne Germain, the foundation's resident representative in Bangladesh at the time, brought in two American bankers as consultants to assess our work. Mary Houghton and Ron Grzywinski, both from the South Shore Bank of Chicago, visited us in Dhaka and in the villages. They were very impressed by what they saw.

"I need a flexible fund," I told Adrienne in 1981. "I need a fund that I can use to cope with the problems we face in our daily work. I also want to offer a guarantee to the commercial bankers who are supporting us so that they can't back out of the expansion by arguing that it is too risky."

With recommendations from Ron and Mary, the Ford Foundation agreed to provide us with $800,000 as a guarantee fund. I assured them we would never need to dip into it. "The fact that it is there," I said, "will do the magic."

And that is exactly how it worked. We put the funds in a London bank and never withdrew a pound.

We also negotiated a loan of $3.4 million from the International Fund for Agricultural Development (IFAD), based in Rome. This amount, matched by a loan from the Bangladesh Central Bank, would be used to expand Grameen's program in five districts over the following three years.

So in 1982, we launched our expansion program to cover five widely separated districts: Dhaka in the center of the country, Chittagong in the southeast, Rangpur in the northeast, Patuakhali in the south, and Tangail in the north. By the end of 1981, our cumulative loan disbursement was $13.4 million. During 1982 alone, our disbursements increased by an additional $10.5 million.

CHAPTER
SEVEN

A Bank for the Poor

Is Born

Though Bangladesh has a population of 120 million, it is run entirely by a handful of people, most of whom are college or university friends. Time and again this unfortunate feature of Bangladesh society and politics has helped Grameen overcome otherwise impossible bureaucratic hurdles. A. M. A. Muhith, for example, had been the economic counselor to the Pakistan Embassy in Washington, D.C., while I was teaching in the United States. During the War of Liberation, we collaborated in lobbying the U.S. government and trying to create public support in the United States for our cause. We were friends.

In 1982, we met again at the Bangladesh Academy for Rural Development in Comilla, where I was supposed to present a paper about the future of the Grameen Bank Project. As we assembled in the conference hall, it was announced that a coup d'état had toppled the civilian government and that the army chief of staff, General Hussain Muhammad Ershad, had assumed power. Martial law was declared. As we were not permitted to leave the building and all meetings had been banned, Muhith and I sat in the cafeteria of the academy with all the other delegates and chatted.

Muhith had become an admirer of Grameen when he was still a civil servant. He had even hoped to start a Grameen program in his own village. Stuck in the conference room, I spent most of the day explaining to him my dream of making Grameen an independent bank and how government civil servants and the bureaucracy of the Central Bank were against me. By the end of the day, the military relaxed its restrictions on public movement, and we returned to Dhaka.

In the following few days, Muhith was unexpectedly named finance minister by the new government. And so it turned out that my day "wasted" in the academy had a determining influence on Grameen. Several months later, I met Muhith and asked for help. He offered to put Grameen's case on the agenda at the next monthly meeting of the Central Bank. It was a difficult meeting. Muhith faced a storm of opposition from the managing directors of all the government-owned banks, who came up with a dozen reasons why it would be unwise to turn Grameen into a separate bank.

After the meeting, Muhith took me aside and asked, "Yunus, do you have patience?"

"Yes, that is all I have," I said.

"Good, well, let me handle this my way."

A couple of months later, Muhith again convened a meeting of the seven managing directors through whose branches we had been administering the Grameen project. Again he raised the issue of the future of Grameen. And again all said that the work that Grameen was doing was impressive but converting us into an independent bank would be disastrous.

One managing director said, "Yunus will have to bear a lot of administrative costs that right now he can pass on to us. He doesn't realize the time and expense his type of poverty banking requires."

Another said, "Yunus, why don't you create a division of our bank and work through us? Wouldn't that suit you better?"

"No, it would not," I said. "I would have to adapt to the rules and procedures of your bank. In Tangail, we have seen that is extremely difficult. Nearly impossible."

"You will lose money," warned another managing director.

In my Boy Scout uniform at age 13, in 1953

My first US apartment,
Nashville, 1966

With my wife Afrozi
at our wedding reception,
April 1980

Meeting with borrowers at
the Ruhea Thakurgaon branch
in Dinajpur

Loan disbursement at the branch
office at Shashiddhi, Sri Nagar

Fish cultivation and group meetings
of Grameen Fisheries Foundation
in Nimgachi

Fabric-making at Grameen's Araihazar
and Sadipur branches

Clockwise from upper left:
rope making; cotton dying; cotton spinning;
weaving; embroidery work

Livestock raising at Shaharail Singair branch;
Leasing; Grameen Health Activities

A village "telephone lady"
with a Grameen cellular phone

With former President Jimmy
Carter, Afrozi, and my daughter
Deena, receiving the World Food
Prize in Des Moines, Iowa, 1994

Hillary and Chelsea Clinton with
Grameen borrowers in Grameen
village Rishipara, Bangladesh, 1995

World Bank President James D.
Wolfensohn and Mrs. Wolfensohn
visiting Grameen Bank's
Soliabakpur Banaripapra Branch.
Minister Tofail Ahmed and State
Minister A.K. Faizul Huq
are also present.

"It will never work," said another.

"The staff will start cheating you. You don't know what it is to have internal controls. You are not a banker; you have never run a bank. You are a professor."

Fortunately for us, the secretary of the Finance Ministry, Mr. Syeduzzaman, was another friend of Grameen. Muhith enlisted his support and took my proposal directly to the president. As a military dictator, the president had no political legitimacy and perhaps he saw in Grameen a chance to score some political points. Whatever his thinking, it worked in our favor. With the president's blessing, it was a mere formality to present the proposal in the cabinet. The cabinet approved it without raising any new issues, and the Ministry of Finance was awarded the responsibility of implementing the plan.

I wanted the new Grameen Bank to be 100 percent owned by the borrowers. That is how I had been presenting my case all along. But Finance Minister Muhith was convinced that my proposal would have a better chance of passing if I offered a block of shares to the government. Seeking help, I approached Dr. Kamal Hossain, a former foreign minister and senior aide to Bangladesh's first president, who had played a central role in drafting Bangladesh's constitution.

A great admirer of Grameen, Hossain immediately took over all the details of drafting our legal framework. He suggested we offer 40 percent of our shares to the government and keep 60 percent for our borrowers. We went over countless drafts, discussing each paragraph, line, and word in exhaustive detail. Finally we submitted our draft to the ministry.

In late September 1983, while I was on a tour of Rangpur, I received a call saying that the president had signed the proclamation and that the Grameen Bank was born. That was a day of rejoicing. My tiny project in Jobra had grown into a formal financial institution! But back in Dhaka, when I finally read the full text of the proclamation, I was shocked to see that the ownership percentages had been reversed—the government had kept 60 percent of the ownership and the borrowers had been granted only 40 percent. In effect, Grameen had become a government-owned bank. I felt betrayed.

The first thing I did was to call the finance minister. A patient man, Muhith sympathized with my position. "Yunus, I know you are angry at me," he began. "But you wanted to have a bank, didn't you? This was the only way I could get it for you."

"But this is contrary to everything I was working for," I said.

"No, it is not. I have a very clear plan for your bank. I didn't want to get shot down. If I had presented the proposal your way, it never would have gotten through the cabinet. So I changed it to make it easy for the cabinet to approve. Now you go ahead with the task of setting up the bank. Once it is established, you can come back to the Finance Ministry to change the ownership structure. That will be a much easier task. I promise you that within two years I'll get the ownership ratios reversed. You have my word."

I was not quite convinced. I went back and discussed the issue with my colleagues. We all felt we had no choice and that, like it or not, the Grameen Bank was born. We had better take what we had and steer it in the right direction.

Grameen's operations as a full-fledged independent bank began immediately. We signed loan agreements with all the commercial banks to take over our portion of their assets and liabilities effective October 1, 1983. Our first working day fell on October 2. We decided to have an opening ceremony.

We invited Finance Minister Muhith to be the chief guest at our opening. But when we told the ministry staff that the ceremony would be held in a branch located in a village, they replied that the location would not be appropriate and that the festivities should take place in Dhaka so that all the top government officials could attend. I tried to explain to them that Grameen did not operatc in urban areas and that it made no sense to have a ceremony in a place where we had no borrowers.

"If the ceremony were held in Dhaka, it would exclude our borrowers, those who now own 40 percent of the bank." I said. "They can't be transported to the city simply because government officials do not want to come to a village!"

We stood firm in our position. We wanted the function held in a rural setting—where we worked, surrounded by our borrowers, near their homes and their villages. We were a bank of the rural people, for the rural people, and the symbolism of where we opened would not be lost on anyone.

The Finance Ministry official responsible for the Grameen Bank warned us that the minister might not attend the ceremony if we insisted on holding it in a village. I told him that it was up to the minister to decide whether he found the time or not, but that we would go ahead with our ceremony as planned. As the deadlock continued, I called Muhith and told him about our date, the place, and the order of events. He immediately declared that he would attend and gave me the names of several friends who should also be invited. It now became clear to me that it was never the minister, but rather a ministry official, who thought the ceremony should be held in the city. When I mentioned this, Muhith said, "He is crazy. Why should the *Grameen* ("Rural") Bank have its opening ceremony in the city? I cannot even imagine such an absurd thing."

■

When we were drafting the legal framework for the bank, I was also trying to come up with a Grameen logo. In meetings I often scribble or doodle in my notepad. Now my doodles all concerned possible logos. Three themes occupied me, all of them rural. One involved weaving, particularly weaving with cane, which I thought was a beautiful allegory for the way in which tiny pieces can be assembled into a strong whole. I tried many designs with weaving patterns, but none really worked. Another theme was the number five, since all our groups are made up of five borrowers. I tried many arrangements with five sticks, five people, five hands, five faces. The third theme was that of a village hut. It was simple in design and stood eloquently for all that is rural.

At this time, whenever I visited a Grameen village, I carefully noted all the unfinished cane work, the rice husking, the different types of work people did, their shelters, their implements and decorations, to see if I could pick up some detail that I could use in our new logo. I was attending a seminar in Bangkok when the outline of a logo hit me. Rather than paying attention to the lecture, I was working on the theme of the hut. Suddenly out popped a design. I drew several versions of it. One I liked right away. I knew I had found my logo and I even wrote down its color scheme.

As soon as I returned to Dhaka, I had the logo drawn and colored and showed it to Muzammel, Mahbub, Dipal, Nurjahan, and Daiyan. Their response was cautious. They asked many questions. What does it symbolize? What do the colors mean? I gave my own interpretation: The logo's hut stood for the rural but could also be read as an arrow shooting upward, with the red color of the arrow signifying speed. The green at the center of the hut stood for new life, and that was the goal the arrow was aiming toward.

At first my colleagues were not entirely enthusiastic. I argued that we should adopt the logo immediately and put it everywhere—on our letterhead, envelopes, pamphlets, and all other stationery—so that it would become part of the project and be inherited by the new bank. To make the logo an even more inseparable part of Grameen, I suggested we use it on the opening day at our ceremony. We would build a magnified logo out of bamboo and colored paper. It would serve as a gate through which to enter the Grameen branch.

We held the opening ceremony in a big open field in the village of Jamurki in Tangail. We invited groups of borrowers and all the staff from several branches to participate in the ceremony. They filled the field. Other guests came from Dhaka. Minister Muhith, representatives of the borrowers, and I sat on the podium. It was a wonderful day, full of bright sunshine. We began the ceremony with recitations from the holy Quran, as is customary on such occasions, and emotional speeches from the women borrowers. For all of us who had labored so long and so hard to achieve this, it was a dream come true. I looked out over all those women seated in their colorful red, green, ocher, and pink saris—a sea of saris— these hundreds of barefoot borrowers who joined our celebration. They had voted with their feet. There was no doubt about their commitment and their determination to break free from poverty. It was a beautiful spectacle, powerful in all respects.

■

The challenge of transforming Grameen from a pilot project operating inside a mostly hostile banking system to an independent bank for the poor thrilled me as well as my colleagues and our borrowers. We continued to encounter skepticism from Bangladeshi bankers, but from October 2, 1983, onward we could argue our side as a peer institution—and one that was financially outperforming traditional commercial banks. Most important, independence allowed us to grow. We added new branches at a breathtaking rate. I had such confidence in our training methods and in the basic soundness of our micro-lending methodology that I saw no need to go slowly at this point.

Not only did we undergo quantitative growth, but we made many improvements to our methodology in the second half of the 1980s. Until then our staff had been recruited on a temporary basis and had to continually worry about whether the project would

be terminated and they would be out of a job. When Grameen became an independent bank, they were automatically named permanent staff of the new organization. This was the greatest victory
for all of them. We also popularized the Sixteen Decisions, resolu-
tions adopted at a national workshop of borrowers (see Chapter
8), integrated housing loans into our program, expanded our social development efforts, and experimented with irrigation loans
and other seasonal loan programs. Though there were setbacks,
such as the floods of 1987 and 1988 and a repayment crisis in the
district of Tangail (our first), it was a time of growth, innovation,
and confidence. But we realized that for our growth to be sustainable, we needed to resolve some governance issues that were left
over from our campaign to become an independent bank. The
most pressing issue was how to transform Grameen from a bank
owned by the government to one owned primarily by the people
who borrowed from it. We were counting on Muhith to guide us
through this process.

Unfortunately for us, Finance Minister Muhith resigned in
1985 before he had a chance to keep his word about altering
Grameen's corporate structure. But luckily, the permanent secretary of the Finance Ministry, Syeduzzaman, was a close friend of
Muhith's and shared his enthusiasm for Grameen. Syeduzzaman
was also aware of Muhith's promise to me. When I reminded him
about this unfinished business, he assured me that he would stand
by Muhith's decision.

He did. Very quietly, he changed the ownership structure of
Grameen by granting 75 percent of the shares to the borrowers
and keeping 25 percent for the government, the government-
owned Sonali Bank, and the Bangladesh Krishi (Agriculture)
Bank.

But there were other complications that came with our governmental status. In 1986, the composition of the board of directors
was altered to bring in the majority members from the borrower-

shareholders. We now found ourselves in a strange situation. Grameen became a private bank run by a "government official." According to our legal framework, I was a government-appointed managing director. As such, I had to follow all the rules of a civil servant, including asking permission from the president before I could leave the country to attend any meetings. One particularly aggravating incident came in 1985, when I was not able to attend the UN women's conference in Nairobi. My request for permission to leave the country was rejected by the president, who raised the question, "Why should a man go to a UN women's conference?"

My appointment also hung from a very weak thread. The official letter of appointment said that I was "managing director until further orders." In other words, I occupied my position as long as the government was not unhappy with my work. I could wake up one morning and read in the newspaper that somebody else had been appointed as managing director of Grameen in my place. The government was not required to explain why I had been dismissed or what I was supposed to do with myself.

This organizational arrangement did not ensure stability. I kept worrying that one government or another would suddenly replace me, and plunge Grameen into a crisis. And so I consulted the lawyer who had helped us set up the bank, Dr. Kamal Hossain. We worked out a request for an amendment to the Grameen legislation by the parliament. It had to be brought to the floor of parliament through the Finance Ministry. But officials in the ministry were in no mood to get this provision amended. Why should they help to change the provision that gave them unlimited power to remove the managing director? I sent in my proposal for amendment and, as expected, the Finance Ministry paid no attention to it. I then maneuvered to place it with a higher body called the Executive Committee of the National Economic Council, a body of ministers. They recommended that my proposal be adopted. Still, the permanent secretary of the Finance Ministry paid no attention. When I raised the issue with him personally, he argued that the council was not the government and that the Ministry of Finance was not required to take instructions from the council. For me, this was an unforgettable lesson in the obtuse functioning of the government machine.

I kept knocking at any door I could find. Finally, I raised the issue with President Ershad himself. He ordered his finance secretary to put my proposal up for consideration at his next cabinet meeting. But the finance secretary sent the papers to the president with a recommendation not to amend the provision. I did not give up. I explained my case to the secretary in charge of the presidential Secretariat. This senior bureaucrat happened to have been a student in my math class while I was teaching at the University of Colorado in Boulder. When I asked for his help, he promised to do everything possible. He organized a high-level meeting on the issue, inviting the vice president, the governor of the Central Bank, the finance minister, the finance secretary, the planning minister, and myself. The president was to preside at the meeting.

I argued my case as forcefully as I could. Everyone in the room expressed support for my position except for the finance secretary, who built his case around the fear that the government would lose the ability to properly supervise the bank. Despite his warnings, the meeting approved the amendment proposal. It was finally sent to parliament and passed just before the parliament was dissolved and the Ershad government brought down by a people's uprising. Under the new provision, a managing director had to be appointed by the board of directors, not by the government. Once the board went through the legal steps and appointed me managing director of Grameen, I stopped being a government servant and became an employee of the bank. More important, the Grameen Bank was now free to choose a CEO who would serve the interests of its shareholders and not stand at the mercy of the government.

The amendment was a crucial alteration in the Grameen Bank legislation. But to further ensure the future of the Grameen Bank, there is another vital issue that still needs to be addressed. This relates to the appointment of the chairperson of the board of directors, which is currently assumed by the government. Again, in the usual government style, the appointment is valid only "until future orders," that is, the chairperson can be deposed by the government any time. This arrangement threatens the bank's stability. The role of the chairperson is crucial, particularly as nine of the thirteen members of our board of directors, representatives of the borrowers, are usually illiterate.

■

Through the 1980s, Grameen's aggressive expansion program saw us adding approximately one hundred new branches every year. These new branches were of very high quality as six years of experimentation in Jobra and Tangail had taught us a great deal and allowed us to refine our methodology. By 1985, we had an impressive cadre of young professionals with several years of village experience behind them who were able to guide and manage hundreds, and later thousands, of new recruits. We experienced some problems in our oldest branches in Chittagong and Tangail, where our borrowers had been subjected to many changes in policies as we went through our process of trial-and-error, but branches started during or after 1983 performed extremely well.

We originally located our nationwide headquarters in Shymoli, then something of a suburb of Dhaka, outside the city's financial district. I tried to postpone our move to the capital city—where powerful bureaucrats seem to inevitably lose touch with the rural reality—but by 1983 we had no choice. Still, I insisted that everyone make a solemn commitment to stay true to our rural grassroots origins. We decided that no one should work in the head office who had not spent several years working in one of our rural branches, a rule that we have only broken a handful of times over the past fifteen years.

As we expanded, we watched our borrowers progress through successive loan cycles. In most cases, the size of their loans increased as their businesses and their self-confidence grew. Some of the most dynamic borrowers used their profits to build new houses or repair existing homes. Every time I visited a village and saw a house built with profits from a Grameen-financed business, I felt a thrill, but I still regretted that more borrowers were not able to undertake such major investments. I began to think about how we could create a new program that would offer dependable borrowers with perfect repayment records long-term loans for house building or repairs. I imagined that this new loan program would begin as a kind of a reward to exceptional borrowers. But I was unsure about how to proceed. Then, in 1984, I noticed an advertisement by the Bangladesh Central Bank announcing a new refinancing plan for housing loans in rural areas. In response to this advertisement, the Grameen Bank applied to the Central Bank for help in introducing a housing program to its borrowers. We explained that we were constrained by the modest circumstances of our borrowers, who could not repay sums of money as large as those mentioned in the Central Bank's ad. Our borrowers could not take out 75,000-taka (about $2,000), but we did want to extend 5,000-taka ($125) housing loans to them.

The Central Bank rejected our application. Its experts and consultants decided that whatever one built for $125 would not satisfy the structural definition of a house. Specifically, they said that such a house would not add to the "housing stock of the country."

I protested. "Who cares about the 'housing stock of the country?'" I said. "All we want are leak-proof roofs and dry spaces for our members to live in."

We tried to make the Central Bank consultants see what a major improvement even this minimal housing would be over our borrowers' current situation, but our arguments were all in vain. They would not budge.

Then we came up with another idea. We sent in a second application, explaining that we no longer wanted to make housing loans but rather "shelter loans." We were hoping they did not have a definition or statistic for "shelter stock" that would disqualify us. But though the consultants in charge of the project showed no objection to our shelter loan idea, the economists in their group argued that our borrowers could not afford non–income-generating loans. Grameen was doing fine work with loans for income-generating endeavors, or "productive activities," as they called them, but shelter loans were "consumption items." Our borrowers could not afford loans that did not generate income to help them pay off their debt.

And so we went back to the drawing board. This time we said that we wanted to offer our borrowers "factory loans." We explained that the overwhelming majority of our borrowers were women and that they worked from the home. "Our borrowers look after their children while they work and they earn money from their work," I explained. "Most of this activity is performed in their own homes. Since their homes are places of work, we choose to call them factories. Furthermore, the monsoon plagues them for five months out of the year. During that time they can't work because they don't have sturdy roofs over their heads. To continue to work and generate income, they need protection from the rain. That is why we want to offer them factory loans. True, this 'factory' will double as a house, but more important, it will have a direct impact on their income-generating ability as it will allow them to work throughout the year with some comfort."

The consultants rejected our application for a third time. I arranged for a personal meeting with the Central Bank governor to ask him to override his bureaucrats.

"Are you sure the poor will repay?" the governor asked.

"Yes, they will. They do. Unlike the rich, the poor can't risk not repaying. This is the only chance they have."

The governor of the Central Bank looked at me. "I'm sorry you had difficulties with our officials," he said. "On an experimental basis, I will allow Grameen to introduce a housing loan program. Good luck."

■

To date, we have extended a total of $190 million in loans to build more than 560,000 houses with near-perfect repayment in weekly installments. The housing programs of the conventional commercial banks cannot boast such success. Few of their borrowers paid their loans back and the program was discontinued after three years. Our housing program continues to this day and is expanding.

Our position was also vindicated when Grameen's housing program was chosen in 1989 by a jury of some of the top architects in the world to receive the Aga Khan International Award for Architecture. At the awards ceremony in Cairo, distinguished architects kept asking me who the architect was who had designed our prototype, a compact $300 house.* I answered that no professional architect ever designed the houses built by our borrowers. It is the borrowers who are the architects of their own houses—as they are the architects of their own fate.

---

*By 1989, the size of our typical housing loan had grown to $300.

CHAPTER

EIGHT

Growth and

Challenges

for the Bank

for the Poor,

1984–1990

Bangladesh has long attracted people who study population-related issues. They tell us that we are poor because there are too many of us on too small a piece of land. Approximately the size of Florida, Bangladesh has a population of about 120 million. If half of the U.S. population decided to move to Florida, those people would experience the population density we now have in Bangladesh. What does all this mean for Bangladesh? Should we curtail birth rates?

I believe there is a strong element of fear mongering in population policies promoted by international development agencies. We in the Third World often blindly echo these views, raising even more fear at home. Since Bangladesh became an independent country, our population has almost doubled. But we are certainly not twice as poor. Indeed, we are better off today than we were twenty-seven years ago. We have fewer food shortages and though we feed twice the population we are far more self-sufficient in food grains.

My suspicion is that governments and international agencies choose to scare people into action to distract attention from their own ineptitude. Rather than limiting population growth, they should concentrate on improving the economic status of the people in general and the people at the bottom half in particular.

Governments and population agencies are not putting nearly as much effort into changing the quality of life of the poor as they put into their scare tactics, such as pressuring illiterate men and women to physically remove their ability to procreate.

UN studies conducted in more than forty developing countries show that the birth rate falls as women gain equality. The reasons for this are numerous. Education delays marriage and procreation; better-educated women are more likely to use contraceptives and more likely to earn a livelihood. I believe that income-earning opportunities that empower poor women and bring them into organizational folds will have more impact on curbing population growth than the current system of "encouraging" family planning practices through intimidation tactics. "Family" planning should be left to the family.

The Grameen Bank is often cited in population discussions because the adoption of family planning measures among Grameen families is twice the national rate of Bangladesh. During the Cairo Population Conference of September 1994, it was also noted that the birth rate among Grameen families is significantly lower than the national average. Once they have increased their incomes through self-employment, Grameen borrowers show remarkable determination to have fewer children, educate the ones they have, and participate actively in our democracy. If micro-credit can help bring family-planning awareness to families, why do not governmental and international agencies, which are so concerned about population growth, promote micro-credit more actively than they do? Could it be because micro-credit runs as a profit-oriented business? Are there vested interests in the current population programs? I believe that the emphasis on curbing population growth diverts attention from the more vital issue of pursuing policies that allow the population to take care of itself. The sooner we rearrange our priorities, the better it will be for all people on the planet, now and in the future.

■

I first began to see societal problems being solved, one Grameen family at a time, during annual workshops we held for center leaders at each branch. These workshops gathered together center leaders to review their problems and achievements, to identify areas of concern, and to look for solutions to social and economic challenges. The workshops worked so well that we held a national workshop of selected center leaders in 1980 in Tangail. At the end of it we wrote down four decisions resolved on by the group. We did not expect these decisions to be taken more seriously than the proceedings of the meeting, but we soon started getting requests for copies from centers throughout Bangladesh.

At our second national session in 1982, we concluded the workshop with "Ten Decisions." These ten decisions were increased to sixteen in our 1984 workshop in Joydevpur. We never imagined how deeply these decisions would affect our members. Today, at every Grameen branch, our members take enormous pride in reciting the Sixteen Decisions. They are as follows:

1. We shall follow and advance the four principles of the Grameen Bank—discipline, unity, courage, and hard work—in all walks of our lives.

2. Prosperity we shall bring to our families.

3. We shall not live in a dilapidated house. We shall repair our houses and work toward constructing new houses at the earliest opportunity.

4. We shall grow vegetables all the year round. We shall eat plenty of them and sell the surplus.

5. During the plantation seasons, we shall plant as many seedlings as possible.

6. We shall plan to keep our families small. We shall minimize our expenditures. We shall look after our health.

7. We shall educate our children and ensure that they can earn to pay for their education.

8. We shall always keep our children and the environment clean.

9. We shall build and use pit latrines.

10. We shall drink water from tube wells. If they are not available, we shall boil water or use alum to purify it.

11. We shall not take any dowry at our sons' weddings; neither shall we give any dowry at our daughter's wedding. We shall keep the center free from the curse of dowry. We shall not practice child marriage.

12. We shall not commit any injustice, and we will oppose anyone who tries to do so.

13. We shall collectively undertake larger investments for higher incomes.

14. We shall always be ready to help each other. If anyone is in difficulty, we shall all help him or her.

15. If we come to know of any breach of discipline in any center, we shall all go there and help restore discipline.

16. We shall introduce physical exercises in all our centers. We shall take part in all social activities collectively.

Now in our national workshops, I plead with the participants not to increase the number of decisions. I argue that we should concentrate on doing a good job implementing the existing Sixteen Decisions rather than adding new ones. Local branches of Grameen, however, may formulate decisions that address problems specific to their areas. These decisions are a demonstration that the poor, once economically empowered, are the most determined fighters in the battle to solve the population problem, end illiteracy, and live healthier, better lives. When policy makers finally realize that the poor are their partners, rather than bystanders or enemies, we will progress much faster than we do today.

■

Bangladesh is a land of natural disasters. This is an unfortunate but unavoidable factor in our business. But no matter what cataclysm, weather disaster, or personal tragedy befalls a borrower, our philosophy is always to get that person to pay back his or her loan, even if it is only at the rate of a half penny a week. This discipline is meant to boost the borrower's sense of self-reliance, pride, and confidence. To forgive a loan can undo years of difficult work in getting that borrower to believe in his or her own ability.

If a flood or a famine decimates a village and kills borrowers' crops or animals, we immediately lend them new money to start up again. We never wipe out old loans, but convert them into very long term loans and try to get the borrower to pay them off more slowly and in smaller installments. In the extreme case where a borrower dies, we disburse funds from the Central Emergency Fund (a life insurance fund for borrowers) to the deceased's family as soon as possible. We then ask the group or center to adopt a new member from that same family to bring the group number back up to five.

Bangladesh has so many natural disasters that one area may be hit by several in the same year. It has happened that a village, a district, or a whole region is hit by floods as many as four times in one year, which can completely wipe out all the savings and assets of a family. We experienced severe flooding in 1981, 1985, 1987, and especially 1988, when our plight was broadcast overseas by the international media. There were also localized disasters, such as the tornado that hit the Manikganj District in 1989. Grameen's operational procedures in such situations are always the same. First, we suspend all rules and regulations of the bank. The local bank manager and all bank personnel are directed to immediately scour the region to save as many lives as possible and to provide shelter, medicine, food, and protection. Second, the bank workers visit the houses of our members and try to reestablish the victims' confidence by letting them know that the bank and their fellow members are ready to support them. We then find out what the survivors need and make provisions to provide it. We provide emergency food as well as water and saline solution to prevent dehydration and diarrhea. Emergency seeds for planting and cash for buying new cattle and new capital assets are also distributed. Disaster loans are provided. We want to give our members time to mourn their loved ones, but we do not want them to sink into apathy and lethargy from despair. We want them to start right up again thinking of survival schemes. Because national and international relief is usually late and inadequate, the only way that victims can get through the pain, suffering, and devastation is by rebuilding what they had. During periods of disaster, old loans are rescheduled and a grace period is accorded for repayment. In a special meeting, the local center is given the authority to decide how long this grace period should last. We also look into longer-term plans that will make the area safer, such as building cyclone shelters. Many of our Grameen branch offices along the coast are now built in solid, reinforced concrete.

Grameen keeps no overall statistics on how many natural catastrophes it has had to overcome, but I estimate that about 5 percent of our loans go to survivors of natural catastrophes. Pramila Rani Ghosh's story illustrates the kind of disasters that often confront our borrowers. In 1971, during the War of Liberation, Pramila's house was burned down twice by the Pakistani army. She joined Grameen in 1984. In 1986, she contracted enteritis and went into Tangail hospital. She was operated on and was told not to work for several years. Her fellow group members suggested she take a loan from their group fund to pay for her operation, but as there was not enough money, she sold her cow and her grocery shop.

She was given a new loan with which she bought milk cows. When these died of an unknown disease, she went to her weekly center and took out a loan of sixty dollars from the group fund with which she bought a new cow. During the floods of 1988, the village of Chabbisha was under water and Pramila's house was destroyed. She lost all her crops. For three weeks an epidemic raged in the village. The bank staff visited the villagers daily to distribute water purification tablets. Pramila, along with thousands of other Grameen families, received forty kilos of wheat. She paid back the value of that wheat into a center disaster fund. She also bought vegetable seeds from us, which we sold at cost. Three weeks later, when the situation had normalized, she was able to reopen her grocery store.

In 1992, the fire from an oil lamp spread and burned down Pramila's house. Neighbors and villagers tried to help her extinguish the fire, but in the ensuing blaze Pramila lost all her crops, food, her entire grocery store, and her two cows. All that was left were the clothes she and her husband had on their backs. The morning after the fire, the Grameen staff visited Pramila and organized a special meeting at which they offered her a loan from the center's disaster fund. Instead, she decided to take out a seasonal loan and a loan from her group fund. Part of the loan she used to start up a small grocery store and the rest she invested in fertilizer for her irrigated land. With the help of her three grown sons, she was able to start paying off the loan. Three months later Grameen granted her a housing loan, and she constructed herself a new home.

Pramila is currently on her twelfth loan. She owns and leases enough land to feed her whole family and sell about ten maunds of rice paddy a year.

■

From the very beginning, Grameen has gone against traditional methods of poverty alleviation by handing out cash without any attempt to first provide skills training. We have received a great deal of criticism for this policy, even from some of our friends. In Jobra, we simply did not see any need for formal training, and our experience in the 1980s gave us more confidence that we had taken the right approach.

Why give credit first?

I firmly believe that all human beings have an innate skill. I call it the survival skill. The fact that the poor are alive is clear proof of their ability. They do not need us to teach them how to survive; they already know how to do this. So rather than waste our time teaching them new skills, we try to make maximum use of their existing skills. Giving the poor access to credit allows them to immediately put into practice the skills they already know—to weave, husk rice paddy, raise cows, peddle a rickshaw. And the cash they earn is then a tool, a key that unlocks a host of other abilities and allows them to explore their own potential. Often borrowers teach each other new techniques that allow them to better use their survival skills. They teach far better than we ever could.

Government decision-makers, many NGOs, and international consultants usually start the work of poverty alleviation by launching very elaborate training programs. They do this because they begin with the assumption that people are poor because they lack skills. Training also perpetuates their own interests—by creating more jobs for themselves without the responsibility of having to produce any concrete results. Thanks to the flow of aid and welfare budgets, a huge industry has evolved worldwide for the sole purpose of providing such training. Experts on poverty alleviation insist that training is absolutely vital for the poor to move up the economic ladder. But if you go out into the real world, you cannot miss seeing that the poor are poor not because they are untrained or illiterate but because they cannot retain the returns of their labor. They have no control over capital, and it is the ability to control capital that gives people the power to rise out of poverty. Profit is unashamedly biased toward capital. In their powerless state, the poor work for the benefit of someone who controls the productive assets. Why can they not control any capital? Because they do not inherit any capital or credit and nobody gives them access to it because they are not considered creditworthy.

I believe that many training programs are counterproductive. If Grameen had required borrowers to attend a training program in business management before taking out a loan to start a business, most of them would have been scared away. Formal learning is a threatening experience for our borrowers. It can even destroy their natural capacity or make them feel small, stupid, and useless. Also, poor people are often offered incentives to participate in training programs—sometimes they receive immediate financial benefits in the form of a training allowance or training is made a prerequisite to obtaining other important benefits in cash or in kind. This attracts the poor, even though they may not be interested in the training itself.

This is not to say that all training is bad. But training should not be forced on people. It should be offered only when they actively seek it out and are willing to pay in kind or cash to obtain it. Grameen borrowers, for example, do look for training. They might want to read the numbers in their passbooks, for example, or figure out what amounts have been paid and how much remains to be paid back. Often Grameen borrowers want to be able to read the Sixteen Decisions, keep accounts, or follow business news. Or they may want to learn about poultry raising; cattle raising; or new ways of planting, storing, and processing crops. Grameen is also bringing new technology to them: cellular telephones, solar energy, the Internet. Soon borrowers will need to calculate the cost of telephone calls or read the words on a computer screen.

■

Even before I started the Grameen Bank, I had been a critic of international aid agencies in Bangladesh. By far the most influential agency, and the one I have most criticized, is the World Bank. The World Bank and Grameen have been through so many fights and disagreements over the years that some commentators have labeled us "sparring partners." There have always been a few individuals in the World Bank who understand what micro-credit is all about, but our styles are so radically different that for many years we have spent more time and energy fighting each other than helping each other.

One public confrontation occurred at the World Food Day teleconference of 1986. Patricia Young, national coordinator of the U.S. Committee for World Food Day, invited me to be a panelist along with the World Bank's then-president, Barber Conable, at a teleconference that would be broadcast by satellite to thirty countries. I had no idea what a teleconference was, but I accepted the invitation as an opportunity to explain why I felt credit should be accepted as a human right and how credit could play a strategic role in removing hunger from the world.

I had not intended to go into battle against the World Bank president, but Conable provoked me by stating that the World Bank provided financial support to Grameen in Bangladesh. I thought I should correct this erroneous information, and I politely interjected that the World Bank did no such thing. Conable paid no attention. Again he stated that World Bank funds helped Grameen. This time I firmly contradicted him. Conable ignored my protest and repeated that the World Bank provided financial support to the Grameen Bank. I thought I should make the truth clear to satellite-TV viewers. We at the Grameen Bank have never wanted or accepted World Bank funding because we do not like the way the bank conducts business. Their experts and consultants often take over the projects they finance. They do not rest until they have molded things their way. We do not want anyone to come and meddle with our system or to tell us how to behave. Indeed, just that year we had actually rejected a $200-million low-interest loan from the World Bank. I also told Conable, who was bragging about employing the best minds in the world, that hiring smart economists does not necessarily translate into policies and programs that benefit the poor.

I find multilateral donors' style of doing business with the poor very disconcerting. I can cite one example of my experience in the island of Negros in the Philippines. In 1989, a Grameen replication program called Project Dungganon had been launched in response to the growing malnutrition among island children. Several years after it had been established, Dr. Cecile del Castillo, Project Dungganon's founder, asked a UN agency for money to expand her program. The agency responded by sending four missions to investigate her proposal, spending thousands of dollars on airline tickets, per diems, and professional fees. Due to bureaucratic complications, however, the project never received a single penny. In other words, after nearly five years of specialists reviewing the problem and wasting precious resources, the poor islanders were unable to receive a single micro-credit loan with support from this agency. I cannot help but remark that had the Negros project received an amount equal to the cost of a single UN mission, it could have assisted several hundred poor families.

The growth of the consultancy business has seriously misled international donor agencies. The assumption is that the recipient countries need to be guided at every stage of the process—during identification, preparation, and implementation of projects. Donors and consultants tend to become overbearing in their attitude toward the countries they help. Furthermore, these consultants often have a paralyzing effect on the initiatives of the recipient countries. Officials and academics in these countries quickly adopt the figures mentioned in the donors' documents even if they personally know that those figures are incorrect.

■

After 1986, when Grameen made it clear to the World Bank that we would not let it tell us how to run our business, the bank decided to try to form its own micro-credit organization in Bangladesh by combining our methodology with those of a number of other micro-credit programs. I thought the idea was wholly unrealistic. Ultimately, the Bangladesh government took our advice and resisted the World Bank initiative, but the World Bank did not learn anything from the process. On the contrary, it removed the name "Bangladesh" from the rejected project document and offered it to the Sri Lankan government instead.

My less-than-pleasant experience with the World Bank spurred me to learn as much as I could about development agencies. One observation that became increasingly apparent is that multilateral aid institutions have a lot of money to disburse. Officials determine target amounts for each country. The more money officials manage to give out, the better grade they receive as lending officers. Therefore young, ambitious officers of a donor agency will choose the projects with the biggest price tag. By moving a lot of money, their name moves up the promotion ladder.

In my line of work, I have often witnessed the desperation of donor agency officials to give away ever-larger sums of money to Bangladesh. They will do almost anything to achieve this, including bribing government officials and politicians either directly or indirectly. For instance, they will rent newly built, expensive houses owned by government officials or invite them on attractive foreign trips under the guise of official workshops and conferences. Consultants, suppliers, and potential contractors often facilitate this bribing mechanism. After all, they are the ones who most benefit from projects funded by donors.

One research institution in Bangladesh estimates that of the more than $30 billion in foreign donor assistance received in the past twenty-six years, 75 percent was not spent in Bangladesh. It was spent on equipment, commodities, and consultants from the donor country itself. Most rich nations use their foreign aid budget mainly to employ their own people and to sell their own goods, with poverty reduction as an afterthought. The 25 percent that is spent in Bangladesh usually goes straight to a tiny elite of local suppliers, contractors, consultants, and experts. Much of this money is used by these elites to buy foreign-made consumer goods, which is of no help to our country's economy or workforce. And there is a general belief that a good chunk of donor money ends up as kickbacks to officials and politicians who have helped make purchase decisions and sign contracts.

The situation is the same in all countries receiving aid, which amounts to $50–$55 billion a year. Aid-funded projects create

massive bureaucracies, which quickly become corrupt and inefficient, incurring huge losses. In a world that trumpets the superi-
ority of the market economy and free enterprise, aid money still
goes to expand government spending, often acting against the
interests of the market economy.

Most foreign aid goes to building roads, bridges, and so forth,
which are supposed to help the poor "in the long run." The only
people really benefiting from most of this aid, however, are those
who are already wealthy. Foreign aid becomes a kind of charity
for the powerful while the poor get poorer. If aid is to have some
impact on the lives of the destitute, it must be rerouted so that it
reaches poor households more directly.

I believe that a new aid methodology has to be designed with
new objectives. In fact, the direct elimination of poverty should be
the objective of all development aid. Development should be
viewed as a human rights issue, not as a question of simply increasing the gross national product (GNP). When the national economy picks up, the situation of the poor is not necessarily
improved. Therefore development should be redefined. It should
refer only to a positive measurable change in per capita income of
the bottom 50 percent of the population.

■

One day I was approached by an American journalist who was
openly irritated by my apparently endless carping against "development aid" organizations such as the World Bank. Like many
others, he saw the World Bank as a benevolent and enlightened
organization, doing its best at a thankless task. He raised his mi-
crophone in the air between us and said in a challenging voice,
"Instead of always being so critical, could you tell me what concrete steps you would take if you became president of the World
Bank?"

"I have never thought of what I would do if I were president of the World Bank," I said coolly. "But I suppose the first thing I would do would be to move the headquarters to Dhaka."

"Why on earth would you do that?"

"Well, if as Lewis Preston [then president of the World Bank] says, 'The overarching objective of the World Bank is to combat world poverty,' then it seems to me the bank should be moved to a location where poverty is at its worst. In Dhaka, the World Bank would be surrounded by human suffering and destitution. By living in close proximity to the problem, bank officials might be able to solve it faster and more realistically."

The interviewer nodded. He seemed less agitated than at the start of the interview.

"Also, if the headquarters were moved to Dhaka many of the bank's five thousand employees would simply refuse to come. Dhaka is not known for its vibrant social life and is certainly not a choice spot for a World Banker to raise children. I think that many would voluntarily retire or change jobs. This would help achieve two things: First, it would ease out those who are not completely devoted to fighting poverty; second, it would reduce costs, as Dhaka salaries would be much lower than those required in expensive Washington, D.C." And that was the end of that.

In 1987, when I was visiting the United States, I had a much more productive meeting with the American press. I was speaking before a congressional committee. At the end of the hearing, I was rushed to a tiny room where someone was busy talking into a speakerphone. I had no idea how a telephone conference call worked and no one had briefed me, but there I was, faced with a speakerphone and fourteen editorial writers from leading daily newspapers waiting on the line to ask me questions.

The person initially talking on the speakerphone was Sam Daley-Harris. An ex–high school teacher turned social activist, Sam had started a national volunteer network called Responsibility for Ending Starvation Using Legislation, known as RESULTS. Every month he held nationwide meetings with all his volunteers over the phone. What I had stepped into was a press conference. Sam is extremely affable and he spoke in a way that briefed the news writers and me at the same time. I then took questions.

The first conference call lasted for an hour. There was a short break and then another one began with fourteen more editorial writers from various American dailies. That day I learned just how effective RESULTS could be. The resulting editorials helped ensure the passage of legislation in December 1987 that required USAID to devote $50 million to funding micro-credit programs for the poor, despite strong opposition by the Reagan administration.

Sam and I became instant friends. Unassuming and unimposing, he is as solid as a rock when it comes to fighting poverty and hunger. Today, RESULTS has sister organizations in six countries—the United States, the United Kingdom, Canada, Germany, Japan, and Australia. These organizations have endorsed micro-credit as a key antipoverty strategy, and work through their grassroots network of citizen activists to ensure it is noticed by the community, the media, elected representatives, and the national government. They have pushed governmental aid agencies and private agencies for more funding for micro-credit programs. They have lobbied treasury departments and ministries to pressure the World Bank into paying more attention to poverty issues—not just once, but every year since the mid-1980s. They have also campaigned for programs and policies that would reduce poverty in their own countries. In fact, RESULTS in the United States has created a suborganization called RESULTS Domestic that is a leading advocate for micro-credit initiatives in the United States. Over the past ten years, the bond between RESULTS and Grameen has strengthened. Each RESULTS volunteer sooner or later becomes an expert on Grameen.

The 1987 conference calls accomplished another milestone in the history of the micro-credit movement: They attracted the attention of CBS's *60 Minutes.* In 1989, two CBS TV crews, one from London and another from Rome, came to visit Dhaka. I spent long hours with the CBS correspondent Morley Safer, visiting Grameen villages and interviewing borrowers, development experts, and government officials. In all, the crews took over a hundred hours of film footage and boiled it down to just twelve minutes. Broadcast in March 1990, the segment became an instant hit. I had never fully realized the power of the media until then. Even today, we receive letters and phone calls from around the world when the show is rebroadcast. In just twelve minutes, CBS had brought out the essence of Grameen in a most inspiring way. The film moved people to action and activism more than any media coverage before or since.

■

When I talked about micro-credit in the 1980s, whether to World Bank economists or journalists, most people assumed that I was trying to alleviate poverty by lending to small businesses that would then expand and *hire* the poor. It took people a while to see that I actually advocated lending to the poor directly. Policy makers tend to equate job creation with poverty reduction and economists tend to recognize only one kind of employment—salaried employment. And economists tend to focus their research and theories on the origins of wealth in the former colonial powers, not on the microlevel reality of poor people in Third World countries. Whatever attention is given to poverty comes under the rubric of so-called development economics, a field that emerged only after the Second World War and that has basically remained an afterthought or reinterpretation of the main body of economic theory.

Worst of all, economists have failed to understand the social power of credit. In economic theory, credit is seen merely as a means with which to lubricate the wheels of trade, commerce, and industry. In reality, credit creates economic power, which quickly translates into social power. When credit institutions and banks make rules that favor a distinct section of the population, that section increases both its economic and its social status. In both rich and poor countries alike, credit institutions have favored the rich and in so doing have pronounced a death sentence on the poor.

Why have economists remained silent while banks rejected the poor as unworthy of credit? Nobody can provide a convincing answer. Because of this silence and indifference, banks have imposed a financial apartheid and gotten away with it. If economists would only recognize the powerful socioeconomic implications of credit, they might recognize the need to promote credit as a human right.

The shortcomings of the core economic theories remain unchallenged. Microeconomic theory, for example, which plays a central role in the analytical framework of economics, is incomplete. It views individual human beings as either consumers or laborers and essentially ignores their potential as self-employed individuals. This theoretical dichotomy between entrepreneurs and laborers disregards the creativity and ingenuity of each human being and considers widespread self-employment in Third World countries as a symptom of underdevelopment.

In many Third World countries, the overwhelming majority of people make a living through self-employment. Not knowing where to fit these individuals into their analytical framework, economists lump them in a catchall category called the "informal sector." But the informal sector really represents the people's own effort to create their own jobs. I prefer to call it the "people's economy," a term often used by a German friend of mine, Karl Osner, who has played a critical role in educating Europeans about micro-credit. Any economist with a real understanding of society would have come forward to increase the efficiency of this people's economy rather than undermine it. In the absence of economists' support, organizations like Grameen must step into the breach.

CHAPTER

NINE

Applications in Other

Poor Countries

Our success in Bangladesh led me to hope that our micro-credit methodology could have near-universal applicability. During the late 1980s and early 1990s, we proved that the Grameen idea could improve the lives of poor people throughout the world. Pilot projects in Malaysia and the Philippines led the way.

I met Professor David Gibbons, a Canadian who had been living and teaching in Malaysia for more than twenty years, at a conference near Dhaka in 1985. David had been advocating the expansion of credit access in rural Malaysia but was discouraged by the response—or lack of response—among policy makers. He asked me whether he and a colleague might come and spend a month at a Grameen branch. I agreed.

David came to Bangladesh with Sukor Kasim, a junior colleague who would later become one of the most dedicated promoters of micro-credit in Malaysia and around the world. The two spent several weeks in Rangpur shadowing S. A. Daiyan, a zonal manager in one of the poorest areas of Bangladesh. They stayed in villages and toured bank branches. On returning to Dhaka, David and Sukor announced their intention to establish a Grameen program in Malaysia. I fully supported their plan.

When David launched Project Ikhtiar, a Grameen program in Malaysia, in 1987, he encountered challenges on two fronts—

building a Grameen program from scratch and finding an appropriate legal framework to distance the program from governmental control without losing financial support. It was quite a balancing act. David was lucky to have Sukor, a true disciple, as well as Mike Getubig of the Asia and Pacific Development Centre (APDC), who provided seed funding in the early stages of the Malaysia program and later helped fund two of the earliest Grameen replication programs in the Philippines.

When problems piled up, David came back to Grameen for refresher training; on one occasion we sent a team of Nurjahan and Shah Alam, our senior staff, to assist him. Slowly, David and Sukor came to understand the logic of our methodology and modified their policies to more closely resemble ours. By the end of their two-year experimental phase, they announced ambitious plans to expand to even less developed regions of northern Malaysia. Today, David and Sukor are at-large ambassadors for Grameen, working night and day to jump-start Grameen programs in more than a dozen Asian countries. They have been instrumental in forming an association of Grameen replication programs called CASHPOR, and as a result of their efforts Amanah Ikhtiar Malaysia now reaches more than 42,000 poor families, roughly half of Malaysia's population living under the poverty line. The Malaysian repayment rate is even higher than that of borrowers in Bangladesh. David also published a book, *The Grameen Reader*, a compilation of my essays and several of his own articles. This tremendously valuable guide has helped many people adapt our program in other countries.

■

Even before the pilot phase of Project Ikhtiar was complete, serious Grameen replication projects began to crop up in a number of other countries. Three of those showing the most promise were located in the Philippines. Dr. Generoso Octavio, an economics professor at the University of the Philippines at Los Banos, visited Bangladesh in 1989 and started a program in the villages outside his university soon thereafter. As I had joined the board of directors of the International Rice Research Institute, with headquarters located a mere two miles from the Los Banos campus, I was able to visit Gene and his borrowers frequently. With his natural gift for relating to poor people, Gene did a terrific job of getting the project off the ground. Many of his borrowers successfully raised pigs, a very profitable business that is nonexistent in Bangladesh due to Islamic prohibitions concerning the consumption of pork.

At first I thought that operating a Grameen-type lending program in the Philippines would be easier than doing so in Bangladesh, where the long-standing poverty, low status of women, and frequent natural disasters are more extreme. But Gene ran into trouble when, with my encouragement, he set his sights on expansion. He had a knack for working directly with borrowers, but he had more difficulty managing his staff and board of directors. Once his action-research project was converted into an independent micro-credit organization, called Ahon Sa Hirop ("Rise Above Poverty"), or ASHI, he struggled to establish a dependable management structure. After several years of internal battles within ASHI, he left to teach in Malaysia and subsequently become a micro-credit consultant for several organizations with programs in Southeast Asia.

At first I worried about ASHI's future, but then two very fortunate things happened. First, Sukor Kasim stepped in as a consultant to rehabilitate ASHI's most troubled branch. Within a surprisingly short time, things began to look up. Second, an ASHI board member named Mila Mercado volunteered to become the full-time executive director. Mila was a no-nonsense woman with a strong background in the private sector, excellent managerial skills, and a natural talent for working with poor women. Today, due to the efforts of Sukor, Mila, and the ASHI staff, ASHI is one of the most successful Grameen replication programs in the Philippines.

■

Shortly after ASHI got started, I met Governor Daniel Lacson of the province of Negros Occidental, a sugar-growing region in the southern Philippines. We were both in Washington, D.C., attending a seminar held at the World Bank, and everyone was discussing the harm that bank-imposed "structural adjustment policies" were having on poor countries. When it came my turn to speak, I argued that the people losing jobs due to World Bank policies were the "new poor" and that I was more concerned about the "old poor," those who never had jobs in the first place. I did not condone the World Bank's approach, but I argued that the majority of the "new poor" would survive because they had support to fall back on and I urged the attendees at the seminar to turn their attention to the "old poor" instead. I then offered the Grameen-style micro-credit program as an example of how we could help these critical cases.

Inspired by my talk, Governor Lacson sent Dr. Cecile D. del Castillo, the director of a nonprofit organization called the Negros Women's for Tomorrow Foundation, to visit Grameen in Bangladesh. Like David Gibbons, Cecile learned everything she could about Grameen, and in August 1989, she launched a new program called Project Dungganon ("Integrity") in Negros Occidental. With her background in social work and her strong connections to international and national donor organizations, Cecile quickly built up an excellent program serving several thousand extremely poor borrowers. By the early 1990s, Project Dungganon had become the largest program of Cecile's foundation.

■

The third Filipino program to emerge was the Landless People's Fund of the Center for Agriculture and Rural Development (CARD). CARD was established by Aris Alip and a number of energetic people from an organization called the Philippine Business for Social Progress. After visiting Grameen in Bangladesh, Aris decided to apply our methodology to rural development in the Philippines. One member of his staff, Dolores Torres (known as Dory), emerged as the real driving force in the organization. Within a short time Aris and Dory surpassed ASHI and Project Dungganon to become the leaders of a network of more than thirty Grameen replication programs in the Philippines. In 1997— by which time CARD had acquired more than nine thousand borrowers, an excellent repayment rate, and seven branches—the staff took steps to establish the CARD Bank, an independent financial institution. (By January 2003, CARD had grown to 69,000 borrowers.) I was concerned that they were taking a big risk. Rather than base their framework on that of traditional financial institutions, I urged them to create a distinct legal framework from scratch, catering to the needs of micro-credit programs.

Despite its remarkable success, CARD did face some difficulties. In the early 1990s, I looked to the German government to provide it with expansion funding. One German government official responded that his agency considered CARD a failure. Confused, I asked him for the source of his information. He said that a thorough study had been done and everyone who read the report agreed that CARD was not worthy of funding. I asked him for a copy of the report, which he promised to send me.

When I asked Dory about the German evaluation, she said that there had never been one. Then, a few weeks later, she called me to report that a German man, who had not identified himself as an evaluator for the German government, had visited with CARD staff in their head office. He had expressed no interest in visiting with borrowers. This was certainly our mysterious evaluator. I immediately called several people I knew in the German government, but was told that the report was confidential and that I would not be allowed to see it. Frustrated, I approached Dr. Mahabub Hossain, an independent researcher with an impeccable reputation, to do a full evaluation of CARD and then publish the findings. Mahabub agreed to write the evaluation for free. After many long months of painstaking research, he finally presented his findings at an international workshop in the Philippines in June 1997. This is what he discovered:

- CARD borrowers are very poor; 70% of them are completely landless and own houses worth less than $550.

- CARD borrowers use their loans for business; 97% of borrowed money is invested in income-generating activities.

- CARD loans make a big difference; borrowers' average rate of return on investment is 117% (144% for borrowers who have taken five or more loans).

- CARD generates jobs; economic activities financed by CARD loans generated 163 days of employment for CARD borrowers each year and an additional 84 days for other family members.

- CARD generates productive employment; the labor productivity in CARD-financed businesses is 36% higher than the prevailing wage rate.

I had not been expecting such a positive report. CARD was obviously making a tremendous difference to thousands of poor people—transforming their lives even faster than we were able to do at Grameen. But despite Mahabub's findings and CARD's success, the controversy about Grameen's applicability outside of Bangladesh, or even in the Philippines, was not put to rest. A new report released by the United Nations in 1998 repeated many of the old arguments about why micro-lending programs can work only in places with certain unique characteristics. The report argues that "many people, especially the poorest of the poor, are usually not in a position to undertake an economic activity, partly because they lack business skills and even the motivation for business. Furthermore, it is not clear if the extent to which micro-credit has spread, or can potentially spread, can make a major dent in global poverty."*

Encouraged by the success of the programs in Malaysia and the Philippines, new programs continued to sprout up in India, Nepal, Vietnam, and elsewhere. Even China launched three programs in the mid-1990s. Then came Latin America and Africa, with a program called the Small Enterprise Foundation (SEF), founded by John De Wit in South Africa. John's program has been particularly successful, reaching thousands of poor borrowers in rural villages. One of his borrowers, Kate Makaku, now makes a living by selling avocados, mangos, bananas, cheese snacks, and soft drinks from a small store. Before joining SEF, Kate sold her wares door to door, but she had very little capital, which severely limited profits. Kate's story is illustrative of the travails and successes in the Third World outside of Bangladesh.

Kate got into business when, shortly after her marriage, she realized that the money her husband sent home from his work in the mines was not enough to last her through an entire month. Rather than starve, she took the money and bought mealie meal, a food staple in South Africa, as well as avocados and sugar, and sold them to people in her neighborhood. Her sales allowed her to squeak by, but when her husband was injured at work and unable to return to the mines, Kate's situation became desperate.

*United Nations General Assembly, 53rd Session, *The Role of Microcredit in the Eradication of Poverty* (A/53/223, 10 August, 1988).

It was at about this time that she joined a SEF group. With her initial loan of sixty dollars, she made a down payment on a used refrigerator, allowing her to open a store. The other women in her group also set up small businesses. Sylvia Moagi raises chickens and sells milk from her home. Grace Motlousi is a fruit vendor. Masaku Maenetja sells paraffin and has a home-based sewing business. Rebecca Sebiya brews beer.

Even though her workday starts at 3 A.M., Kate is happy that her life is finally on the right track. Her customers clamor for her bestselling "fat cakes" and business is brisk. Kate's latest loan was for $300 and she is having no trouble paying it back. She even has enough saved up to lend money to her husband for his new carpentry business. Though her work leaves her little extra time, Kate has enrolled in an adult literacy program. For the first time, she can now sign her own name.

The opportunity to catch up with borrowers like Kate always makes it difficult for me to decide which Grameen replication programs I should visit when I travel—the ones I have visited before, to see how they have grown, or ones that I have not yet visited, to find out how various organizations have adapted our policies to their cultural context. We now send many middle-level and senior Grameen staff members to help people create new programs, alter existing ones, or expand.

■

In our discussions with the first wave of Grameen replicators, we found that many organizations had a hard time mobilizing financial support for their activities. They needed funds to travel to Bangladesh for training, to start up their programs, and then to expand after the pilot phase. I urged replicators to look for sources of funding in their home country—the closer to their office, the better. That way, they would be able to keep all financial transactions in their country's currency and directly demonstrate the impact of their work to their funding agencies. But despite my encouragement and occasional intervention—I sometimes contacted agencies to recommend funding for particular countries—some of the best programs kept coming up empty.

One day I was complaining about this situation—billions of dollars for Third World development, but none for dozens of good micro-credit programs—at a lecture in Chicago. During the question-and-answer session I elaborated on how difficult it was to start replication programs because of the lack of donor money. My suggestion was to create a branch of the Grameen Trust specifically for providing support to replication programs. If donors were satisfied with the use of their money, they could give us more. If they were unhappy with our performance, they could remove their support.

As the question-and-answer period continued, I was handed a note from someone in the audience. It said, "Can I see you for a couple of minutes after your presentation?" I passed the note to Connie Evans, executive director of the Women's Self-Employment Project, who was sitting next to me. Immediately after the lecture, Connie ushered me into a small room. A woman was also shown in.

"How much money do you think you'll need to start funding the replication projects?" asked the woman.

"A couple of hundred thousand dollars would be a good start," I answered.

"Will you have difficulty in finding replication projects to fund?"

"Oh, no. There are many that are waiting for money," I answered. "And once we start funding, many more will come forward."

"How long will you be in town?"

"Another two days. Then I go to Washington."

"I'll try to give you a check for couple hundred thousand dollars before you leave. Can I invite you to my home this evening so that you can meet a few of my colleagues and we can proceed with the processing of the grant?"

I looked at Connie and asked, "Can I go?"

Connie was beaming with excitement. "How can I stop you from going to Adele Simmons's home, particularly when she wants to give you a grant?"

That evening we spent with Adele, the president of the MacArthur Foundation, and three of her colleagues, who agreed with Adele's decision to offer us a grant. As I had a hectic schedule for the next two days and no time to write a grant proposal, Adele assigned a staff member to hop into taxis with me, sit next to me during lunches and dinners, and develop a draft of the proposal during my stay. Within two days, the staff had written a proposal that satisfied the MacArthur Foundation.

Adele Simmons's decision to support the Grameen Trust jump-started us on our ambitious new replication program and encouraged other donors to follow suit. These included the Rockefeller Foundation, the World Bank, the U.S. government, the UN Capital Development Fund, and the German government. In total, the Grameen Trust—which has been run by a former Chittagong University colleague and close friend of mine, H. I. Latifee, since 1994—has received more than $19.8 million. Virtually every cent has been used to support sixty-five Grameen replication projects in twenty-seven countries. As of late 2002, these organizations have granted more than $444 million in loans to some 1,140,000 poor people.

Grameen attracts potential replicators by inviting them to our International Dialogue Programs—two-week-long conferences hosted by the Grameen Bank and Grameen Trust in Bangladesh four times each year. About twenty people from around the world attend each conference. After a few hours of orientation in our head office, we send these visitors in groups of two to far-flung branches throughout the country. They remain there for five days to learn as much as possible about the branch, its workers, its borrowers, and its socioeconomic environment. They then undertake an in-depth interview with one Grameen borrower over several days. This allows them to see the direct impact of Grameen on a very human level. It also helps to break down the myths and prejudices the participants may have about poor people in Bangladesh, poor people in their home country, or poor people in general.

When the Dialogue participants return from the field, we encourage them to debate the merits and limitations of the Grameen approach. Toward the end of the two-week period, we show them how to apply to the Grameen Trust for seed money to get their own program started. If they apply, we contact other replicators in their country for references. All of this is very inexpensive, but it allows us to weed out those who are not serious about starting a program true to the Grameen spirit. We see a tremendous demand for new funding and hope to reach 10 million borrowers through replication programs funded by the Grameen Trust by 2005. That goal will require roughly $2.2 billion. This may sound like a lot of money, but it is less than double the amount that an American friend of mine helped raise for his law school a few years ago.

■

About eight years ago a fellow Bengali challenged me in a seminar. He said, "Grameen once received loans at 2 percent interest. Any program in this country that gets loans at that rate can make a micro-credit program work." I think he meant it as an accusation, implying that what we had accomplished was not a big deal, but I took it as a challenge to create a new institution that offered loans at 2 percent interest to any micro-credit program in the country. I convinced the government to establish a nongovernmental agency, called the Polli Karma-Sahayak Foundation (PKSF), which has since made loans to 156 micro-credit programs throughout the country. I was appointed to the board of directors. After PKSF established a track record and methodology that felt comfortable, I supported the proposal that the foundation receive funding from the World Bank. In 1998, the World Bank approved a $105 million loan to PKSF, one of its largest investments in micro-credit ever. Now I believe that several micro-credit "wholesalers" like PKSF should be set up in every country so that they can compete against each other. The retail institutions, and the poor people themselves, will benefit directly from this competition.

In 1993, I circulated a proposal that called for $100 million for Grameen Trust to be used for the support of poverty-focused micro-credit programs that operated on a retail level in developing countries. The response to my proposal, despite lobbying campaigns by RESULTS volunteers in seven countries, was not very encouraging. Then, one evening in 1993, I received a telephone call from the World Bank. It was Vice President Ismail Serageldin. Ismail and I had worked together as steering committee members of the Aga Khan Foundation in Geneva and I knew he was a genuine admirer of Grameen. Despite holding a high position in the World Bank, he had not lost a feel for the poor.

"How can we help? Is there anything we can do for you?" he asked

"Well, I don't know. The World Bank only works through governments. You can't work directly with us," I said.

"No, we very much want to work with you, but you always refuse our money."

"We don't need your money. We can manage our own."

"What response are you getting on the $100 million proposal you circulated for the Grameen Trust?"

"Very frustrating experience. Nobody came forward except USAID with $2 million."

"Did you send a copy of the proposal to the World Bank?"

"No, we didn't. We didn't think you'd be interested."

"Can you fax me a copy tomorrow? I'll see what we can do for you."

The next day I faxed the proposal to Ismail. He called me back about a week later, jubilant. "We checked your proposal. We have good news for you. We want to give you the balance of $98 million."

"I am delighted to hear that. We thought we'd never find this money. But how are you by-passing the Bangladesh government?"

"Don't worry, we discussed that too. We'll find a way."

"Let me get this straight, Ismail—are you talking about a loan or an outright grant?"

"A loan of $98 million," Ismail answered.

"But Ismail, the trust will never be able to pay back a loan."

"This is a soft loan with a very long maturity period. It is almost like a grant," Ismail explained.

"But I know how this works. Soon your official will ask for a guarantee from the government for this loan. And why should our government guarantee a loan to the Grameen Trust, knowing that we will give this money to projects in other countries? The Trust will never recover the original amount even if loan repayment is 100 percent. We make projects responsible only for the local currency equivalent of the loan they receive. When they pay back, they pay back in the local currency. But the World Bank will want U.S. dollars. Because of currency fluctuations, the trust will sometimes receive much less, in dollar terms, than what was loaned. I see no way we can take a loan, even if it is a soft loan."

"I see your point," Ismail said. "What if we give you the entire money up front. Then you can invest it and earn enough to compensate for the losses through exchange rate fluctuations."

"I am not an expert on fund management in the international market. I need an expert," I said. "Why don't you look into the matter and help us draw up a business plan that will protect both the trust and the World Bank."

Ismail promised to do that. But neither his specialists nor the ones I consulted came up with a satisfying scenario. For the time being, the World Bank offered us a grant of $2 million without requiring a government guarantee. This grant did not come from the World Bank's loan fund, but from the president's discretionary fund. To mobilize additional funds for micro-credt programs, Ismail created CGAP, which was established with a $30 million grant from the World Bank.

Though CGAP's first three years were far from perfect, it did a lot of good. Ismail followed Consultative Group for International Agricultural Research (CGIAR) guidelines in designing the structure of the CGAP. He proposed the creation of a Policy Advisory Group, similar to the Technical Advisory Group of the CGIAR, and suggested that I be named chairperson. From that position, I had the opportunity to associate with a diverse group of practitioners and donors working together to set the global stage for micro-credit. It was exciting. Though several of the programs that received funding from CGAP did not seem to place enough emphasis on the poorest, three leading Grameen replication programs—CARD, SHARE (a program in India started with Grameen Trust funding), and Project Dungganon—did receive grants. CGAP was quickly followed by CGAP II in July 1998. If CGAP II can sharpen its focus on the poorest people and adopt a policy to provide most of its funding to national wholesaler funding agencies like PKSF rather than directly funding retailers, I believe its impact will be significant. I also think that a larger percentage of CGAP funds should go directly into the hands of poor women instead of going to consultancies, international conferences, and research studies.

■

In March 1995, a group of volunteers from the citizen advocacy group RESULTS came to visit us in Bangladesh. It was the third such delegation. RESULTS participants pay their own way and are always extremely committed to the fight against poverty. As very few of them are professionally involved in development, they remain untouched by the high salaries and cushy benefits that tend to dull one's compassion for the poor.

During one of the sessions with the RESULTS volunteers, I brought up our proposal for $100 million in funding for the Grameen Trust. Many of the volunteers had lobbied their governments to make contributions to the Grameen Trust, but in most cases their governments had rejected the idea. Sensing the disappointment in the room, I suggested that we shift our focus. What if we found 1 million persons who would each contribute one hundred dollars toward the Grameen Trust's efforts to fund Grameen replication programs? We could call it the People's Fund for micro-credit.

Dave Ellis, an educator and philanthropist based in South Dakota, raised his hand to ask a question. He looked very excited. "When are you going to launch this program?" he asked me.

I looked at my watch and said, "Five minutes ago."

Dave pulled a hundred-dollar bill from his wallet and said, "Well, I'm the first one. Now only 999,999 to go." Suddenly, all the other participants started holding up hundred-dollar bills. Some who did not have their money with them borrowed from others. In a few minutes, I had more than twenty hundred-dollar bills in front of me. It was exhilarating. I announced the People's Fund in *Grameen Dialogue,* our quarterly newsletter, and more checks came rolling in from around the world.

Thrilled by the success of the People's Fund, Dave hired a public relations firm and worked with it to design a campaign logo, website, brochure, and business plan. During several successive trips to the United States, I met Dave and Jeff Swaim (the creative director for the public relations firm Amherst & Reeves) to discuss the campaign. The idea of linking 1 million people in wealthy countries with millions of poor people in developing countries through micro-credit was tremendously exciting to me—not only because of the impact on the borrowers, but also because of the impact on the donors. It would create thousands of people-to-people links and indirectly educate millions about the potential of micro-credit.

Understandably, Dave did not want to process all the hundred-dollar checks through his small, Rapid City–based foundation. So Reed Oppenheimer, a philanthropist and RESULTS activist, agreed to establish a U.S.-based nonprofit organization called Grameen Foundation USA (GF-USA). Reed paid all the legal costs of setting up GF-USA and based it in his home state of Oklahoma. As we contemplated the campaign's move from Dave's foundation to GF-USA, we recognized an opportunity to establish a broader mandate for GF-USA than simply managing the People's Fund. So I asked Alex Counts, an American who had been associated with us in Bangladesh for nearly ten years and who had written a book about Grameen entitled *Give Us Credit,** whether he would move back to the United States to become the executive director of GF-USA. He agreed. Reed became the chairperson of the board, Alex moved to Washington where GF-USA's main office would be located, and Jeff and Dave continued to work on the campaign.

To date, we have only raised $142,000 through the People's Fund and are still trying to raise the funds needed to implement our business plan. Our goal is to raise the campaign budget separately, so that 100 percent of each hundred-dollar contribution goes through the Grameen Trust and on to grassroots micro-credit

*New York: Times Books, 1996.

programs—with neither GF-USA nor the Grameen Trust retaining any percentage for their administration and overhead. If we can find some foundation, company, or individual willing to fund the plan that Dave and Jeff came up with, I am sure Alex could multiply that amount many times and in a reasonable amount of time generate $100 million in hundred-dollar increments.

■

We have come a long way from the days when we did not know whether Grameen could function outside of Bangladesh. Dozens of projects in countries with very different cultures, climates, and levels of development have shown how versatile our micro-credit methodology really is. We have tried our best to spread the word about the power of micro-credit and help people who want to start or expand their own projects abroad. To conserve our energy, we have concentrated on projects with a strong poverty focus, but we are convinced that our model can work among nonpoor populations as well. Despite these successes, we have only begun to scratch the surface. Millions of families around the world are still victims of unjust economies that do not recognize their right to credit and relegate them to lives of virtual slavery. These are people with untapped potential who suffer the pain of hunger and poverty even though it is avoidable.

Micro-credit is not a miracle cure that can eliminate poverty in one fell swoop. But it can end poverty for many and reduce its severity for others. Combined with other innovative programs that unleash people's potential, micro-credit is an essential tool in our search for a poverty-free world.

CHAPTER

TEN

*Applications in
the United States
and Other Wealthy
Countries*

Whenever I am asked if Grameen can work in other countries, I respond emphatically that it can work wherever there is poverty, including in wealthy countries. Poor people throughout the world are worthy of credit. The initial interest of many American individuals and organizations in Grameen led me to believe they might try to replicate our program for the benefit of the poor, the homeless, and the unemployed in the United States. I was not prepared for the amount of skepticism I encountered. What struck me was not so much people's doubt as to whether micro-credit would succeed in the United States but their pessimism about whether *anything* would actually raise people out of poverty rather than merely alleviating its symptoms. Many Americans argue that their welfare state has created a lazy underclass of dysfunctional individuals who would never be interested in or capable of starting their own businesses or supporting themselves. I knew Americans—not just wealthy or educated Americans, but Americans generally—to be remarkably resourceful people and I was surprised by their skepticism. I decided to keep my eyes open for anyone interested in giving micro-credit a try.

It was not until the mid-1980s that people in the United States began showing real interest in applying Grameen principles to their own poverty problems. I suppose it all began in 1985, when

Bill Clinton, then governor of Arkansas, was looking for ways to create new economic opportunities for the low-income people of his state. Hillary Rodham Clinton's college roommate, Jan Piercy, had just returned from working in Bangladesh with an American organization and was at the South Shore Bank of Chicago. She introduced the Clintons to Ron Grzywinski and Mary Houghton, Chicago-area bankers who had done much to convince the Ford Foundation to support Grameen.

■

Ron and Mary advised Governor Clinton that a Grameen-type program could be an answer to the poverty problem in his state. They suggested that he set up a bank designed specifically for the poor in Arkansas. The governor was intrigued and he invited me to Arkansas. On my next trip to the United States, in February 1986, Ron and Mary arranged for us to meet. Governor Clinton was attending the annual Governor's Conference in Washington, D.C., and so we met in the Four Seasons Hotel—Governor Clinton, Hillary Rodham Clinton, Ron, Mary, and myself.

Bill Clinton is a man of voracious curiosity. He wanted to know everything about Grameen—how it got started, how it works, and why nobody had tried it in the United States. As I spoke, both the governor and his wife were drawn into my story. After half an hour, Mrs. Clinton declared, "We want it. Can we have it in Arkansas?"*

"Why not?" I said. "If the governor is committed to it, how can it not happen?"

*Hillary Rodham Clinton's support for the Grameen idea has never diminished. She visited us in Bangladesh in April 1995 and she has visited microcredit programs on three different continents. She also cochaired the Microcredit Summit of 1997.

Clinton turned to Ron and asked him how long it would take to get the program started. Ron explained the steps necessary—all the legal clearances and permissions—concluding that it would certainly take at least six months.

The governor was impatient. "That's too long," he said. "Can't this be done any faster?" He turned to me as if seeking my help.

"If you want me to, I can start it tomorrow morning," I said.

Clinton gave me a broad smile. "Can you really do it? That's what I want. I want you to do it."

I explained my plan. To avoid the legal complications, we would set the bank up as a simple credit program. Ron and Mary would then buy the bank as one of their projects. In the meantime, we would start organizing the borrowers. I promised Mrs. Clinton and the governor that I would visit Arkansas to present an outline of the project after meeting with state officials, potential borrowers, bankers, academics, and business people.

The following week I got my first taste of Arkansas. State government officials made elaborate preparations for me to meet with small business owners. Ron and Mary accompanied me. I was introduced to a local radio station owner, a fast-food operator, a retail outlet manager, and a drugstore worker. But at each successive stop, I became more and more withdrawn. These were not the people I needed to meet. The Clintons had told me about the widespread poverty in their home state, but I was not seeing any of the poor people I was supposed to help. None of these people were really poor. I was looking for poor people.

I expressed my frustration to the state officials. "These are the smallest businesses in the area," they explained. "We don't have any poorer businesspeople."

"No, no," I said. "I don't want to meet poor businesspeople. I want to meet just plain poor people."

They looked at me as if I had spoken to them in Bengali. Obviously they did not quite know what to do or where to take me.

"Do you have welfare recipients in this state?" I asked. "Perhaps there is an office that administers your welfare program with lists of people who receive benefits?"

"Yes, we do have such an office," they answered.

"O.K.," I said. "Let's get the welfare list and start visiting the people who are on it."

My hosts made a few quick phone calls.

It was at this point that our trip began to get interesting. I was taken to meet with welfare recipients. I asked one group, "Suppose that your bank were to lend you money to start a business. How much money would you ask for?"

The room was silent. No one seemed to understand the question. Finally, one person said, "I don't have no bank account."

"But what if you did have a bank account?" I said.

Again, silence.

"What if you had a bank account, and your bank were to lend you money. What would you do with it? Can anyone tell me? Doesn't anyone dream of starting a new business? Doesn't anyone have a hobby that might help earn some cash if done full time?"

I went around the room asking each person individually. I wanted to gauge the interest of the American poor in self-help and self-employment. Critics had predicted that micro-credit would have trouble in the United States because, whereas Bangladesh has a long tradition of self-employment, less than 10 percent of Americans work for themselves. They argued that Americans typically required lengthy and intensive training before they were ready to go into their own business. This sounded contrary to the "can-do" spirit I had always witnessed in the United States, among rich and poor, black and white, Asian and Latino alike. In my gut, I believed such criticisms underestimated the average American. Every day I read about white-collar and blue-collar workers being fired by their longtime employers. It seemed clear to me that future generations would grow accustomed to having two or three different careers in the span of one lifetime and that self-employment would become more common. So I was eager to see how Americans trapped in poverty, some for two and three generations, would react to our offer of credit.

The fear and incomprehension on the faces of those poor people in the community center of a small town in Arkansas was the same as I had seen countless times in Bangladesh. So I spoke as calmly and naturally as I could.

"Look, I run a bank in Bangladesh that lends money to poor people," I said. "And last week, I had a meeting with your governor. He asked me to bring my bank to your community. I am considering starting a new bank right here in your town. I have come today to find out if any of you would be interested in borrowing money from me."

I heard some chuckles in the crowd. It was obvious the people in the room did not really believe me. I went on: "My bank is a special bank for the poor. It requires no collateral and no credit check. All I need is someone unemployed or on welfare who has an idea of what he or she would do with the money. But if there is no business for such a program, why would I open my bank here? I could go somewhere else and give loans to poor people in some other community. That is why I am asking if any of you have any ideas of what you might do with a loan."

One woman, who had been listening carefully, raised her hand. Afraid that I might not notice her, she called out, "Hey, I'd like to borrow from your bank!"

"O.K." I smiled. "Now we are in business. How much would you like?"

"I would like $375."

Everyone laughed.

"What do you want this for?" I asked.

"I am a beautician and my business is limited because I don't have the right supplies. If I could get a nail-sculpting box that costs $375, I am sure I could pay you back with the extra income I'd earn."

"Would you like to borrow more than that?" I asked.

"No, I wouldn't want to take a penny more than what the box actually costs."

Another woman raised her hand and said, "I've been unemployed ever since the garment factory closed and moved to Taiwan. I need a few hundred dollars so I can buy myself a used sewing machine. I want to make clothes and sell them to my neighbors."

Another woman raised her hand. "I want $600 to buy a pushcart so I can sell my hot tamales in the street. My tamales are famous in my neighborhood. If I had a pushcart I could sell them better."

Every suggestion gave me reason to hope. These business plans and aspirations of really poor Americans had a great deal in common with the poor of Bangladesh, Malaysia, and Togo.

■

The Grameen pilot project in Pine Bluff, Arkansas, was put in the hands of Julia Vindasius, an MIT graduate and second-generation American of Lithuanian descent. Julia was working at the South Shore Bank when I met her. She was young, but extremely able, and I suggested she be put in charge of the pilot project. Everybody was surprised by my recommendation. Julia had never been to the South in her life.

The project was originally named the Grameen Fund, but we soon discovered that the name Grameen complicated matters and made Ron and Mary waste a lot of time explaining the history of Grameen and Bangladesh. One day in my office in Dhaka, I received a call from Mary in Chicago. She recommended that the project be renamed the Good Faith Fund, suggesting that the bank does not rely on collateral but rather on the good faith of its borrowers. Of course, Good Faith Fund made a lot more sense. It was simpler and easier to understand.

The Good Faith Fund slowly grew to reach hundreds of low-income people in Arkansas. When Clinton ran for president, he often used it as an example of a successful, innovative means to fight poverty. At one point Clinton announced his intention to start a nationwide network of micro-credit programs modeled on the Good Faith Fund. This prompted many telephone calls and letters from the United States.

During a 1992 interview with the editors of *Rolling Stone* magazine, Clinton spoke particularly fondly of Grameen. In a separate article, two of the editors ridiculed him for being too ready to promote micro-credit in the United States. I was disappointed, but an American friend explained that *Rolling Stone*'s reaction was hardly surprising. He argued that Grameen was a "Third World technology transfer" and that the American elite might not be ready for it. Given the reluctance of Americans to adopt successful policies from countries as close to them as Canada, Germany, or England, it would prove very difficult for Clinton to convince his fellow Americans to follow a Bengali model.

As president, Clinton continued to take a personal interest in the Good Faith Fund in Arkansas and to support micro-credit. But unfortunately, since the election of a Republican Congress in 1994, he did not spend much political capital placing micro-credit on his national agenda. Nevertheless, he continued to visit micro-credit borrowers on his international trips during and after his presidency and his vocal support has spurred the creation and expansion of many micro-credit programs.

■

My experience in Arkansas was repeated in many parts of the United States. In South Dakota, I stayed with Gerald Sherman, director of the Lakota Fund, and his wife and two children. Gerald trained at Grameen in Bangladesh in 1988. He and the rest of the staff of the Lakota Fund, a leading micro-credit program assisting Native Americans, are members of the Sioux Nation. They showed me the beautiful quilts made by Native American women who used to have no economic opportunity but now receive micro-loans, hold their meetings in churches and community centers, and sell their goods themselves.

In Oklahoma, a most impressive tribal leader, Chief Wilma Mankiller, also took an active interest in the Grameen program. When I visited the Cherokee territory, I met with a group of about twenty poor Cherokee women. Their faces were absolutely expressionless. I told them about Grameen, and they just sat there stoney faced and silent.

I said, "Well, your reaction here is far more encouraging than anything I have ever encountered in Bangladesh. There, women actively try to avoid me. They would run away from me, saying, 'No no, we do not want or need your money.' We would run after them, but still they refused to listen. At least you are seated here and are listening to me. That is extremely encouraging."

No one laughed.

"Does anyone in this room need money?" I asked.

No answer. No hand lifted. No eyes moved.

"If you don't need any money, would you happen to know of a neighbor or a friend who might need some?"

After a long silence, a hand was raised. "Yes, I have a neighbor who I think could use some money," said one woman.

"To do what?"

"To buy himself a little stove on wheels so he can sell tacos."

"And is he good at that? Does he know how to make tacos?"

"Oh, yes," said the little woman. "He is the best taco maker in the area. Everyone loves his spicy meat and crispy tortillas."

"Well, send him around. I am certain we could give him money. Does anyone else have a neighbor or a friend who needs money?"

The Cherokee women in the room all thought for a while, then another hand was raised. "I know that people in this area love puppies."

"Yes?"

"Could I get a loan to raise and sell puppies?"

"Well, if you think you could succeed economically and that you could earn enough to pay back a loan, why yes, of course we could lend you the money. How much would you need?"

"Well, I don't know. To get a kennel, to advertise, and to buy dog food, I suppose I would need $500 for my first litter."

"Well, now we are in business. I will lend you $500."

"You agree! Just like that?"

"Just like that."

Everyone in the room started laughing. I could see people's eyes lighting up. Others were now raising their hands and sharing their money-making ideas.

"I would like to sell potted plants," said one. "I have a green thumb. Everything I touch grows well."

"Do you own land?" I asked.

"That is no problem. Here on the reservation, there is no private ownership of the land. It is free to anyone of the tribe who wants to use it properly."

"And do you think you could sell potted plants?"

"Oh, yes, that would be easy."

We came to an agreement for that loan, and I could see the others in the room scouring their brains for creative new ideas. By the time I left that meeting, they were all asking, "Yunus, when are you coming back? Bring money next time!"

■

Ron and Mary were not satisfied with simply helping the rural poor. Soon they set their sights on urban America. Some years earlier, they had bought an ailing community bank in a poverty-ridden area of Chicago. The South Shore had been abandoned by white storeowners and white-run businesses because blacks were moving into the neighborhood. Slowly, their South Shore Bank won back the community's confidence, acquired new depositors, and began lending to individuals whom traditional banks had avoided.

When the Ford Foundation needed some independent bankers to appraise my proposed guarantee fund, Ron and Mary were asked to visit Bangladesh to evaluate the Grameen Bank. From the outset, they loved what we were doing and hoped to accomplish the same in the ghettos of Chicago.

In 1985, at the request of Ron and Mary, I visited Chicago for the first time. I was invited to talk to social activists, economists, bankers, and community leaders. Almost everyone I spoke with dismissed what I said, arguing that the Bengali experience could not be relevant to poverty eradication in the United States. They claimed that Chicagoans needed jobs, training, health care, and protection from drugs and violence, not micro-loans, and that self-employment was a primitive concept lingering only in the Third World. Low-income people in Chicago needed money for rent and food, not for investment. They had no skills anyway.

I advanced the same arguments I had made to bankers in Bangladesh. "The poor," I said, "are very creative. They know how to earn a living and how to change their lives. All they need is opportunity. Credit brings that opportunity. Perhaps our two societies are different and thousands of miles apart, but I don't see any difference between the poor of Bangladesh and the poor of Chicago. The problems and consequences of poverty are the same."

No one seemed convinced. Only Ron and Mary believed in me. Mary took the lead in establishing the Women's Self-Employment Project (WSEP), a nonprofit organization that over time implemented a variety of innovative antipoverty programs. Among them was the Full Circle Fund (FCF). Started in 1988, FCF offered low-income women access to investment capital of $300 to

$5,000 if they agreed to join a group of five peers and were able to present a sound business proposal. The credit rating or access to collateral of the prospective borrowers was not taken into account during their loan approval process.

Connie Evans, executive director of the WSEP, and Susan Matteucci, a recent MIT graduate, were new to the micro-credit business, but very willing to learn. Before launching the FCF, Connie and Susan came and lived in Grameen villages, spending long sessions with our field staff and zonal managers. When they returned to Chicago, they followed our Grameen handbook to the letter.

It worked, but there were frustrations. Through the FCF, I witnessed directly how welfare laws in the United States create disincentives for welfare recipients to work. Those who receive welfare become virtual prisoners not only of poverty but of those who would help them; if they earn a dollar, it must be immediately reported to the welfare authority and deducted from their next welfare check. Welfare recipients are also not allowed to borrow money from any institutional source. In fact, under the then-existing laws of Illinois, micro-credit programs such as the FCF could not approach welfare recipients at all. WSEP had to negotiate with the welfare authority to get a special dispensation. I was brought to the state welfare authority to testify that credit can help people get off welfare and that they should consider giving welfare recipients who become members of the FCF a waiver from the law for an experimental period of three years. After protracted negotiations, the state of Illinois approved a one-year waiver. Subsequently, this waiver was renewed on an annual basis. Now, thanks to the success of the FCF, the law in Illinois has been amended to allow people on welfare to borrow money.

Defying all conventional advice, the FCF made a bold start. Skeptics argued that the five-woman group idea would not work because Americans are too naturally independent. Not only did the peer system work, it worked in one of the toughest neighborhoods of inner-city Chicago. To encourage prospective borrowers to form groups, the FCF organized regular "parties" to help people get acquainted.

I was invited to meet the borrowers, visit their homes, and join them in celebrations once the FCF was well under way. In the faces of the poor people in Illinois, I saw the same excitement I had seen in the eyes of village women in Tangail. I heard the same expressions of self-discovery, the same aspirations, the same warmth in their voices. Of course, these urban Americans were not raising chickens or husking rice, but they knew what they could do to earn an income. They were confident in their skills and I was impressed by their creativity. One borrower used her loan to buy ingredients, bake, and sell coffee cake. Another, known for her storytelling, produced audiotapes of her stories and sold them in neighborhood stores. Two other borrowers designed and sold clothes in a jointly rented store.

One particularly moving experience I had in Chicago occurred while I visited WSEP borrowers in a Hispanic neighborhood on the West Side. I was shocked to hear that the English language had basically disappeared from the area. All I could hear was Spanish, and as I could not speak a word, I became doubly dependent on the bilingual WSEP staff members who toured with me. They took me to meet several members of their borrowing groups.

One of those members, a frightened-looking woman in her early forties, spoke only Spanish. I told her, "These are beautiful quilts and embroidered designs you make. When did you think of starting a business with this?"

Through an interpreter she explained her life to me in great detail: "When Jenny [a staff member of the WSEP] came and talked to me, I was scared. I thought she is going to try to sell me something. I avoided her. She came back another time with another woman, a Hispanic woman from the neighborhood. They tried to talk to me, but I was still too afraid to listen. They were talking about business. I had no understanding of business. My husband has a hard life. He works in a factory. He gets very angry if I ever try talking to outsiders. He does not like me to leave the apartment by myself. I didn't know anybody in Chicago. I had been living here with my husband for the past fifteen years since I came from Mexico.

"Jenny kept coming back. She told me about the Grameen Bank in Bangladesh—a faraway country. She told me how women in that country changed their lives. I liked the stories she told me, and I wished I could be like the women in that country. But here things were so rough. I did not dare do anything by myself. My husband would kill me if I created trouble for him.

"I started talking to Jenny. She introduced me to other women in the neighborhood. I listened to them. They told me about their hard lives, about their children, about their husbands, about their parents, their brothers and sisters, their childhood. I saw how alike we all were. We talked about Jenny and about the WSEP and about the Grameen Bank. We began to imagine what we might do with loans. We encouraged each other and collected information for each other. Finally, we formed a group. Two by two we took loans. We helped each other in business. I have paid back my first loan of $600. Now I am in the middle of my second loan. I took $1,000 the second time."

"Do you have problems in selling your products?"

"No, not at all. I am behind in filling my orders. I could sell much more, but I do everything alone by hand. I have nobody to help me. My son goes to school. He is always out. I am the only one home."

"Are you happy with the income you make?"

She remained silent for a long time. Then in a whisper, she started talking very slowly. I assumed that she was saying that the money was not much but it helped her—something like that. When she stopped speaking, the interpreter said in English, "I never expected that I would ever earn money. My husband never gives me any money to spend. We shop together. He pays. I never had money of my own. For the fifteen years that I have lived in America, I have never even had a bank account. Now I have money and I have my own bank account. I have a checkbook. My husband does not know anything about it. I have not dared to tell him yet."

I did not know what to say. To hide my emotion I asked, "Many people tell me that if WSEP did not insist on forming groups it would be so much easier for people to borrow. Do you agree?"

She looked at me when the interpreter translated the question and replied softly, "In the fifteen years I have been here, I never had a friend. I didn't even know anybody. I was all alone. Now I have many friends. My four friends in the group are like my own sisters. Even if the WSEP did not give us money, I would not leave the group."

Her eyes filled with tears. She covered her face with both her hands while the translator relayed her words.

■

Alex Counts originally came to Grameen as a Fulbright scholar in 1988. In 1996, he wrote a book, *Give Us Credit,** comparing the impact of Grameen in a village in Bangladesh with that of the Full Circle Fund. Because he spoke both English and Bengali fluently, he was able to immerse himself completely in the lives of borrowers in both cultures. He collected so many interesting stories about micro-credit's effect on women's lives that the first draft of his book was more than 600 pages. After many painful editorial decisions, it was reduced to about 350 pages. It is the most fascinating storytelling I have ever read.

*New York: Times Books.

Today Alex is the president of the Grameen Foundation USA (GF-USA), the Washington, D.C.–based nonprofit organization discussed in Chapter 9 that jump-starts Grameen-style micro-credit programs in places such as Tulsa, Oklahoma; Dallas, Texas; and Harlem in New York City. As members of many organizations in the United States, Canada, and Latin America cannot imagine traveling to Bangladesh, we direct them to GF-USA.

There are also many U.S. programs that have taken the micro-credit idea and adapted it. Some do not require borrowers to form groups. Others do not target the poor. Many do not focus on women. Quite a few offer only business training, as opposed to credit. These organizations, some 250 of them, have formed a network called the Association for Enterprise Opportunity (AEO) to coordinate their activities and hold annual conferences. We keep in close contact with the fifty or so AEO member organizations that operate along Grameen principles as well as the many other AEO members that use alternate approaches to micro-credit.

■

Micro-credit has also succeeded in Europe, both in wealthy Western European countries that suffer from high unemployment and in the poorer Eastern European nations now emerging from Communist rule. But though many European charitable organizations, not to mention intellectuals, bankers, and journalists, are interested in our ideas, few are willing to initiate micro-credit programs themselves. I have addressed German parliamentary committees in Bonn and the German Council of Bishops. I have appeared before French TV audiences and received honorary degrees in England, but still people refrain from real action.

Maybe Grameen upsets too many preconceived European ideas. In the developed world, my greatest nemesis is the tenacity of the social welfare system. Over and over, our clones have run into the same problem: Recipients of a monthly handout from the government feel as afraid to start a business as the *purdah*-covered women in Bengali villages. Many calculate the amount of welfare money and insurance coverage they would lose by becoming self-employed and conclude the risk is not worth the effort.

Some borrowers do try to take loans in secret, hoping the government will not find them out. But government inspectors are often quick to track down any entrepreneurial welfare recipients and immediately remove their state benefits. In industrialized countries, "informal businesses" are akin to illegal street hustles. To be legal, the self-employed poor must file documents, petition bureaucracies, and keep accounting books. It is wholly unrealistic to expect an inexperienced, relatively uneducated person to satisfy all the requirements of a bureaucratic state. As a result, many of our first borrowers from Grameen-type programs in Europe are technically lawbreakers. They are counseled to get paid under the table and to keep their loans off the books.

Often, even when the law allows a poor person to own a business, charity program operators will not allow it. One young man, newly out of prison, wanted to start up a french fries stand. The Parisian charity that housed him would not accept this independence. Instead, it opened its own food stand and hired the man as a salaried employee.

But the situation in Europe is slowly changing. An increasing number of intellectuals and social scientists no longer look to the state as a savior, but turn their eyes to private initiative instead. One such impressive visionary is Rosalind Copisarow, a Polish graduate of Oxford University and the Wharton School of Business, who became a high-powered executive at the J. P. Morgan Investment Bank. Rosalind had never made loans smaller than $100 million when she read a *Financial Times* story on the Grameen Bank during a flight between London and Warsaw. She immediately realized that micro-credit was just what Poland needed. She discussed the idea with Poland's finance minister, who immediately challenged her to quit her job and devote herself to creating a Grameen program there. In December 1993, she decided to accept the challenge. She left J. P. Morgan.

Rosalind and her small team examined two hundred different lending methodologies. They tested nine pilot models. They wanted to adapt Grameen to the traditions of their country. Today they have twenty branches lending to four thousand clients, with a repayment rate of 98.5 percent and loans of $10 million. Rosalind's organization, Fundusz Mikro, intends to be self-supporting with a full banking license.

"When I reflect on my previous career, it seems two-dimensional," says Rosalind today. "It lacked soul. What I do now has put real meaning in my work—and therefore in my life." She is just one of many social entrepreneurs who have devoted their lives to helping provide micro-credit opportunities to the poor.

Another micro-credit visionary is Bodil Maal, who worked in the Norwegian Fisheries Ministry. In 1986, Bodil came to visit her husband, a Norwegian consultant living in Bangladesh. One of Bodil's assignments in the Fisheries Ministry was to encourage young girls who had grown up in the Lofoten Islands to return home. For some years, these islands, situated in a rather desolate spot off the northern coast of Norway, had been experiencing a serious depopulation problem. Though young men often returned to the islands after university, the local girls did not. There was little incentive. While the women waited for their fishermen husbands or fathers to return from sea, there was almost no social or commercial activity to occupy them. They suffered from loneliness. Once the girls began disappearing, young men started to leave too.

A similar depopulation problem was also occurring in northern Finland and in the nearby region of northern Russia. But thanks to the ceaseless efforts of Bodil Maal, the government of Norway decided to initiate a Grameen project through the Fisheries Ministry. This project offered women commercial credit for income-generating activities to help keep them on the islands and make their lives less lonely and more meaningful.

I was invited to visit the projects in northern Norway and was astonished at what I saw: another social transformation, similar in scope to what we are seeing in Bangladesh, but of a very different nature. Now for the first time, the women of the Arctic Circle had access to credit. And thanks to the program, they had access to community support groups and financial opportunities. Currently, they are using their loans to make such diverse items as sweaters, paperweights, postcards, wooden troll statues, and paintings of the local scenery. The work provides them with an important source of income and helps them and their families to cope financially. More important, however, the Norwegian project promotes micro-credit as a tool for social integration and an effective way to add new meaning to people's lives.

Nearby countries have caught on. In Finland, Finnish Microcredit Ltd. has started prototype operations in the Helsinki district. The cooperative Eko-Osuusraha, a "green" credit union, gives microloans to people in ecological and social fields. Four other micro-credit initiatives in rural Finland are governed by the Ministry of Internal Affairs. All of these are based on the model (*nettverkskreditmodel*) begun by Bodil Maal in Norway's Lofoten Islands.

CHAPTER

ELEVEN

Grameen in

the Nineties

In December 1990, the military government that had ruled Bangladesh for ten years was toppled in a popular uprising. The major political parties that had campaigned for a return to democracy agreed to support a caretaker government headed by a former Supreme Court justice. The following February, the caretaker government organized an election that remained mercifully peaceful and resulted in a victory for Begum Khaleda Zia and her Bangladesh Nationalist Party. Sheikh Hasina, the leader of the second largest party, was wise enough to honor Zia's victory. She became prime minister five years later.

In a Third World country like Bangladesh, democracy allows the poor to take advantage of their greatest asset—their large numbers. But to do so, they must be actively organized. I knew how crucial it was that all Grameen borrowers' voices be heard, and I asked our staff to work during the weeks before the 1991 election to ensure that 100 percent of all adult Grameen family members were registered to vote. I also recommended that each center collectively decide which candidate the members would support and that they parade to the voting booths together as a voting block. Even if political office seekers did not take them seriously in that election, they would in the future. I made it clear to everyone that Grameen staff should not attempt to influence which candidates our borrowers supported in any way.

Selecting leaders through democratic means was not new to Grameen borrowers. All Grameen groups elect a chairperson and secretary, and each center chooses a center chief and deputy center chief from among the group chairpersons. So I was not surprised to see how enthusiastically our borrowers embraced the idea of exercising their democratic rights in the national election of 1991. The members of many centers paraded to the voting booths with banners reminding everyone that they were from a Grameen Bank center and were voting as a block. In some cases, local politicians asked if they could address Grameen center meetings.

The real proof of Grameen's influence, however, came after the election, when several defeated candidates came to my office to complain that the Grameen borrowers in their constituency had not supported them. I always told these politicians that they should be talking to the Grameen borrowers, not to me, since I was not the one who cast the ballots.

The election of 1991 also served us as a warm-up for the crucial elections of 1992, 1996, and 1997. In 1992, some four hundred Grameen borrowers were elected to union councils, and in 1996, Grameen borrowers led the way to an almost unthinkable feat— more women voted in the national election than men, which helped to nearly wipe a political party that had taken positions against women's rights out of Parliament. In addition, over 1,750 Grameen members (1,485 female and 268 male) and 1,570 members of Grameen borrowers' families were elected to local offices in 1997. Two Grameen male borrowers and fifty-seven male family members were voted in as chiefs of local bodies. These successful candidates constituted 6 percent of the total elected representatives in all the local bodies in the country. These astonishing results proved to us that once Grameen borrowers grew in self-esteem they would readily express their opinions.

We were so pleased by the results of the February 1991 election and by the continuing expansion of our micro-credit program that we were caught off guard by a series of setbacks that would make 1991 one of our hardest years ever. The first of these hit when the newly elected government decided to forgive all loans from government banks that were under 5,000 taka (approximately $125 at the time). Though this policy may sound as though it would benefit the poor, in reality almost 100 percent of these loans made by government banks went to land-owning, wealthier members of the population. But because most of our loans were also under 5,000 taka, many Grameen borrowers thought that their loans had been forgiven. It was extremely difficult to explain to our borrowers why the rich people in their villages were getting their loans written off but they were not. Yet we had no choice. Grameen did not survive on government subsidies, and writing off all our loans under $125 would have meant the end of us. In the end, our borrowers accepted our arguments, but it was a bitter pill for them to swallow. It is to be hoped that in the future the Bangladeshi government and all governments in countries with micro-credit programs will think twice before trying to garner popularity by forgiving loans.

Even with the loan situation settled, our problems were far from over. On April 30, a cyclone hit the southern region of Bangladesh, killing 110,000 people in one terrible night. The cyclone hit at 2 A.M., catching much of the population unawares. Many Grameen bank workers and managers were badly hurt. After recovering from their shock, those who could went out in boats looking for survivors. Bloated bodies of dead people and animals floated around the flooded remains of former houses.

The survivors were led to dry land. Many of them suffered from severe shock. Fearing that looters would steal their few remaining belongings, some refused to leave their devastated houses. In the hours directly following the flood caused by the cyclone, many traumatized survivors died, as they could not bring themselves to make immediate provisions for shelter and food.

When I arrived in Chittagong to assess the devastation, I was overcome with emotion. One woman told me that she had been running with her child to the cyclone shelter, only to have the child blown right out of her arms by the high winds. After a few minutes, she realized that if she did not enter the shelter immediately she would be killed. She never saw her child again.

We waived all the usual restrictions that apply to housing loans and declared our intention to ensure not just that our borrowers rebuild what they had lost but that they build something better. Many of our borrowers did just that. They also restarted their income-generating enterprises and began making token payments on their loans. It always surprises me how quickly our staff and borrowers are able to recover from natural disasters. Human beings are extremely creative and resilient, especially when they are operating within an institutional framework that encourages and supports their actions. Every time I hear people arguing that Grameen will collapse when another disaster hits Bangladesh, I respond that Grameen and its borrowers will emerge from our rehabilitation efforts stronger than we were before. And every time this has proven to be the case.

■

By 1994, we had fully recovered from the challenges of the decade's beginning and were enjoying our best financial year ever. We had disbanded our donor consortium* the previous year and were operating on purely commercial terms. Two years later, in April 1996, we extended our one-billionth dollar in loans to one

*The donor consortium was formed to coordinate our relations with bilateral and multilateral donors that gave us grants and low interest loans during the 1980s and early 1990s.

of our 2 million borrowers. It was a thrilling moment. A project that had started with a spontaneous twenty-seven–dollar loan from my own pocket had reached its billionth dollar. Just over two years later, we loaned our two-billionth dollar. Grameen was picking up steam.

And when I went to the villages I saw how many of our borrowers had not only crossed the poverty line but left it far behind. I met borrowers whose weekly installment (representing about 2 percent of the loans they were making payments on) was more than five hundred taka ($12)—and heard them tell me that their first loan from Grameen ten years earlier had been five hundred taka. Their capacity to borrow, invest, and repay had increased fiftyfold in ten years.

One such wonderful success story comes from Murshida Begum, who was featured in a PBS documentary on micro-lending called "To Our Credit." Though Murshida's story may strike some as exceptional, it really is a microcosm of what goes on in Grameen—how people are able to reach their full potential much more easily after accessing credit.

Murshida was born into a poor family of eight children. Neither her father nor grandfather owned any farmland. At fifteen she was married to a man from a nearby village who worked as an unskilled laborer in a factory. The first few years of the marriage went relatively well, but things turned sour when Murshida began having children. Just as their family expenses went up, her husband started bringing home less and less money. Finally it became clear that he was a compulsive gambler. During the 1974 famine, he was given a company bonus of 1,800 taka. He lost it all gambling. When Murshida complained, her husband beat her.

To earn some extra money, Murshida took up spinning raw cotton into yarn. She worked on contract for other people and was paid very little, sometimes no more than a handful of broken rice. Still, the work prevented her from starving. She considered other options—working as a domestic servant for a rich family or begging. But what would happen to her children?

One day Murshida's husband came home after a week's absence and complained that there was not enough food for him. Murshida had cooked up something modest and had not eaten the entire day. Angry, her husband beat her and then left, saying he would return later in the morning. That day there was a thunderstorm, and as her husband had sold the roof of their house to pay gambling debts, Murshida and her three children were soaked. At that moment Murshida decided that something had to change. When her husband returned at midnight, Murshida confronted him.

"You have only brought a small quantity of flattened rice for your daughter," she remembers saying, "but nothing for me. Yet everyone in the village says you earn a lot of money." Her husband flew into a rage and beat her. Then he divorced her on the spot and told her to leave the house.

"What about the children?" Murshida asked.

"You can throw them into the river and let them drown, for all I care," he responded.

Murshida sent word to her brother, who offered to take her into his home. Once she had moved in, Murshida found some more work spinning on contract. She heard about the Grameen Bank when it came to her village. Initially, the village leaders opposed Grameen and tried to prevent it from opening centers. One Grameen worker discouraged Murshida from joining, thinking she would move back to her husband's village. But Murshida stopped another bank worker on the village path and begged him to give her money. "I told him I would swim across a river to attend Grameen Bank meetings if necessary. I told him that I wanted to follow him to wherever he was going to form a group, so I could join. I told him that he must give me money, otherwise I would not be able to survive with my children. He said I could not form a group right then, but that he would come to my home and form a group in a few days. And he really came!"

At first Murshida borrowed 1,000 taka to purchase a goat and she paid off the loan in six months with the profits from selling the milk. She was left with a goat, a kid, and no debt. Encouraged, she borrowed 2,000 taka, bought raw cotton and a spinning wheel, and began manufacturing lady's scarves. She now sells her scarves wholesale for 100 taka with tassels and 50 taka without. Murshida's business has grown so much that during peak periods she employs as many as twenty-five women in her village to manufacture scarves. In addition, she has bought an acre of farmland with her profits, built a house with a Grameen Bank housing loan, and set up her brothers in businesses that include sari trading and raw cotton trading. Murshida has also emerged as a leader in her center. She was elected center chief several times.

■

To encourage successful borrowers like Murshida, Grameen started a variety of new loan programs in the 1990s. These included seasonal loans for borrowers who were sharecroppers or who had bought some land since joining Grameen. We also established a tube well loan program for borrowers who needed $50–$100 to sink a hand-powered well to access safe drinking water. Our new family loan program enabled borrowers to take out loans for family members' income-generating projects. And our equipment- and cattle-leasing program allowed borrowers to slowly purchase costly equipment and livestock through a lease-to-own agreement with us. Borrowers used this program to buy such diverse items as videocameras to record the weddings of upper-class people, power tillers and irrigation pumps for cultivation, baby taxis for transportation services, rice mills, photocopy machines, small herds of better-bred cattle, and much more.

Grameen borrowers were constantly branching out into new, creative money-making schemes and we wanted to help them leave the poverty line so far behind that their young children would barely remember what it felt like to be born poor.

Though we wanted to encourage our most successful borrowers to take out bigger and bigger loans, we did not abandon those who were still starting the struggle against poverty. We declared a new goal: to make every Grameen branch "poverty-free" within an allotted period of time.

How did we define "poverty-free"? After interviewing many borrowers about what a poverty-free life meant to them, we developed a set of ten indicators that our staff and outside evaluators could use to measure whether a family in rural Bangladesh lived a poverty-free life. These indicators are: (1) having a house with a tin roof; (2) having beds or cots for all members of the family; (3) having access to safe drinking water; (4) having access to a sanitary latrine; (5) having all school-age children attending school; (6) having sufficient warm clothing for the winter; (7) having mosquito nets; (8) having a home vegetable garden; (9) having no food shortages, even during the most difficult time of a very difficult year; and (10) having sufficient income-earning opportunities for all adult members of the family. We will be monitoring these criteria on our own and are inviting local and international researchers to help us track our successes and setbacks as we head toward our goal of a poverty-free Bangladesh.

■

As I thought more about what we had accomplished at the Grameen Bank, I wanted to convey to other economists and policy makers that our success was not an aberration, but rather a specific example of a new kind of enterprise—an enterprise driven by an attitude that I labeled "social consciousness." But my explanation almost necessitated the creation of a new branch of economics. Traditional theories did little to help me explain what I was trying to do with Grameen.

In my youth, I considered myself a left-of-center progressive because I did not like the way things were, nor did I like the old conservative ways. Like many Bengalis of my generation, I was influenced by Marxist economics. But I also never liked dogmas or groups who told people how to think and what standard practices to follow. I was never an Islamist, but neither could I reject my culture. I never wanted to be so radical that I could not say my prayers or show respect to the Prophet.

Most of my university friends were socialists who believed that government should take care of everything. At Vanderbilt, Professor Georgescu-Roegen, though not a Communist, admired Marxism as a logical construct. So his teaching brought a social dimension to economics. Without the human side, economics is just as hard and dry as stone.

In the United States I saw how the market liberates the individual and allows people to be free to make personal choices. But the biggest drawback was that the market always pushes things to the side of the powerful. I thought the poor should be able to take advantage of the system in order to improve their lot.

Grameen is a private-sector self-help bank, and as its members gain personal wealth they acquire water-pumps, latrines, housing, education, access to health care, and so on.

Another way to achieve this is to let a business earn profit that is then taxed by the government, and the tax can be used to provide services to the poor. But in practice it never works that way. In real life, taxes only pay for a government bureaucracy that collects the tax and provides little or nothing to the poor. And since most government bureaucracies are not profit motivated, they have little incentive to increase their efficiency. In fact, they have a disincentive: governments often cannot cut social services without a public outcry, so the behemoth continues, blind and inefficient, year after year.

If Grameen does not make a profit, if our employees are not motivated and do not work hard, we will be out of business. Grameen, a for-profit bank, could also be organized as a for-profit enterprise of a non-profit organization. In any case, it cannot be organized and run purely on the basis of greed. In Grameen we always try to make a profit so that we can cover all our costs, protect ourselves from future shocks, and continue to expand. Our concerns are focused on the welfare of our shareholders, not on the immediate cash return on their investment dollar.

There is little doubt that the free market, as now organized, does not provide solutions to all social ills. It provides neither economic opportunities nor access to health and education for the poor or the elderly. Even so, I believe that government, as we now know it, should pull out of most things except for law enforcement, the justice system, national defense, and foreign policy, and let the private sector, a "Grameenized private sector," a social-consciousness–driven private sector, take over its other functions.

Almost from the start, Grameen gave rise to many controversies. Leftists said that we were a conspiracy of the Americans to plant capitalism among the poor and that our real aim was to destroy any prospect for a revolution by robbing the poor of their despair and their rage.

"What you are really doing," a Communist professor told me, "is giving little bits of opium to the poor people, so that they won't get involved in any larger political issues. With your micro-nothing loans, they sleep peacefully and don't make any noise. Their revolutionary zeal cools down. Therefore, Grameen is the enemy of the revolution."

On the right, the conservative Muslim clerics said we were out to destroy our culture and our religion.

Wherever possible, I try to avoid grandiloquent philosophies and theories and "isms." I take a pragmatic approach grounded in social considerations. In everything I do, I try to be practical. I rely on learning by doing, while making sure that I am moving toward achieving a social objective.

I am not a capitalist in the simplistic left/right sense. But I do believe in the power of the global free-market economy and in using capitalist tools. I believe in the power of the free market and the power of capital in the marketplace. I also believe that providing unemployment benefits is not the best way to address poverty. The able-bodied poor don't want or need charity. The dole only increases their misery, robs them of incentive and, more important, of self-respect.

Poverty is not created by the poor. It is created by the structures of society and the policies pursued by society. Change the structure as we are doing in Bangladesh, and you will see that the poor change their own lives. Grameen's experience demonstrates that, given the support of financial capital, however small, the poor are fully capable of improving their lives.

Some need only $20, others $100 or $500. Some want to husk paddy. Some want to make puffed rice. Some make earthenware pots and pans, while others buy cows. But—and note this, development specialists around the world—not one single Grameen borrower requires any special training. They either have already received this training as part of their household chores or have acquired the necessary skills in their field of work. All they need is financial capital.

Somehow we have persuaded ourselves that the capitalist economy must be fueled only by greed. This has become a self-fulfilling prophecy. Only the profit maximizers get to play in the marketplace and try their luck. People who are not motivated by profit making stay away from it, condemn it, and search for alternatives.

We can condemn the private sector for all its mistakes, but we cannot justify why we ourselves are not trying to change things, not trying to make things better by participating in the economy. The private sector, unlike the government, is open to everyone, even those not interested in making a profit.

The challenge I set before anyone who condemns private-sector business is this: If you are a socially conscious person, why don't you run your business in a way that will help achieve social objectives?

I profoundly believe, as Grameen's experience over twenty years has shown, that personal gain is not the only possible fuel for free enterprise. Social goals can replace greed as a powerful motivational force. Social-consciousness–driven enterprises can be formidable competitors for the greed-based enterprises. I believe that if we play our cards right, social-consciousness–driven enterprises can do very well in the marketplace.

■

Economic protectionism, subsidies, and welfare benefits were instituted by well-meaning people to soften capitalism's hard edges.

I believe in the central thesis of capitalism: The economic system must be competitive. Competition is the driving force for all innovation, technological change, and improved management.

Another central feature of capitalism is profit maximization. Profit maximization ensures the optimal use of scarce resources. This is the feature of capitalism that led us to create the image of a greedy (almost bloodthirsty) person in the role of profit maximizer. We have presumed that the profit maximizer has no interest in achieving social objectives. We then postulated that true entrepreneurs are a rare and special breed of people whom society should feel lucky to have. We feel so grateful to them that we give them all the privileges we can afford—credit, social recognition, tax holidays, priority access to land, market protection, and so on.

I am proposing two changes to this basic feature of capitalism. The first change relates to this overblown image of a capitalist entrepreneur. To me, an entrepreneur is not an especially gifted person. I rather take the reverse view. I believe that all human beings are potential entrepreneurs. Some of us get the opportunity to express this talent, but many of us never get the chance because we were made to imagine that an entrepreneur is someone enormously gifted and different from ourselves.

If all of us started to view every single human being, even the barefooted one begging in the street, as a potential entrepreneur, then we could build an economic system that would allow each man or woman to explore his or her economic potential. The old wall between entrepreneurs and laborers would disappear. It would become a matter of personal choice whether an individual wanted to become an entrepreneur or a wage earner.

The second change relates to how an entrepreneur makes investment decisions. Economic theory depicts the entrepreneur as only a profit maximizer. Indeed, in some countries, like the United States, corporate law requires the maximization of profits. Shareholders can sue an executive or a board of directors that uses corporate funds to benefit society as a whole rather than to maximize the profits of the shareholders. As a result, the social dimension in the thinking of the entrepreneur has been completely bypassed. For social science and society itself, this is not a good starting point. Even if social considerations have a very small role in the investment decision of an entrepreneur, we should allow them to come into play for the overall social good. A human being's social considerations are qualities that can be inculcated through generating appropriate social values. If we leave no room for them in our theoretical framework, we will be encouraging human beings to behave without respect to social values.

The market, of course, needs rules for the efficient allocation of resources. I propose that we replace the narrow profit-maximization principle with a generalized principle—an entrepreneur maximizes a bundle consisting of two components: (a) profit and (b) social returns, subject to the condition that profit cannot be negative. (Actually, neither of these components should be negative; but I make this conceptualization in order to stay close to the existing profit-maximization principle.)

All investment decisions can be taken within a range of options. At one extreme, the capitalist will be guided purely by the profit motive. At the other extreme, a social entrepreneur will continue to be in the market for as long as his or her socially beneficial enterprise is at least breaking even.

Under this principle, a social entrepreneur could, for example, run a health-care service for the poor if it is financially viable. Other such enterprises might include financial services for the poor, supermarket chains for the poor, educational institutions, training centers, renewable energy ventures, old-age homes, institutions for handicapped people, recycling enterprises, marketing products produced by the poor, and so on.

Would these types of social-consciousness–driven entrepreneurs be rare and difficult to find? I don't think so. The more we look for them, the more we'll meet them and the easier we will make it for a person to become one.

■

I assume that society is made up of many different kinds of people. At one extreme, there are capitalists seeking personal gain who want to maximize profit alone, without social considerations. They would not mind investing in an enterprise that creates negative social returns, as long as it yields a maximum personal profit.

At the other extreme, there are entrepreneurs who are strongly motivated by social consciousness. They are drawn to investments that maximize social returns, provided the enterprises are financially viable.

In between these two extremes, the bulk of entrepreneurs mix profit and social considerations in a way that takes them to their highest level of self-fulfillment. Through various means of social recognition and rewards—I am thinking of prizes, honors, public acknowledgment—societies can influence more and more entrepreneurs to move in the direction of social-consciousness–driven investments.

Specialized institutions can be created to help generate more and more of these investments. An individual entrepreneur can run an enterprise which pays some or no attention to social returns, but she or he can also initiate and operate one or more financially viable enterprises devoted exclusively to maximizing social returns, either as an individual or as a part of a trust or not-for-profit business organization.

This scenario not only brings businesspeople of the future closer to real life, but it also creates room for a socially and environmentally friendly global economy.

Economics must show that a market economy does not necessarily have to be a playground for "bloodthirsty" capitalists; it can be a challenging field for all good people who want to pilot the world in the right direction.

■

Where should one place Grameen philosophy in the spectrum of political ideologies? Right? Left? Center?

Grameen supports less government—even advocating the least government feasible—is committed to the free market, and promotes entrepreneurial institutions. So it must be far right.

Grameen is committed to social objectives: eliminating poverty; providing education, health care, and employment opportunities to the poor; achieving gender equality through the empowerment of women; ensuring the well-being of the elderly. Grameen dreams about a poverty-free, welfare-free world.

Grameen is against the existing institutional framework. It opposes an economy grounded solely on greed-based enterprises. It wants to create social-consciousness–driven enterprises to compete with greed-based enterprises.

Grameen does not believe in laissez-faire. Grameen believes in social intervention without government getting involved in running businesses or in providing services. Social intervention should come through policy packages encouraging businesses to move in directions desired by society. It should provide incentives to social-consciousness–driven enterprises to encourage the competitive spirit and strength of the social-consciousness–driven sector.

All these features place Grameen on the political left.

■

Since Grameen cannot be judged on the basis of its position in relation to the public and private sectors, it is difficult to use traditional political terms to label Grameen. Grameen is opposed to both public and private sectors as they are commonly understood. Instead, it argues for the creation of a completely new sector— what I call the social-consciousness–driven private sector.

Who will or can get involved in this? Social-consciousness– driven people. Social consciousness can be as burning, or even more burning, a desire as greed in an individual human being. Why not make room for those people to play in the marketplace, to solve social problems, and to lead human lives to a higher plane of peace, equality, and creativity?

The public sector has failed. Or at least it is on the way out despite our best efforts. Bureaucratization cushioned by subsidies, economic and political protection, and lack of transparency is killing it off. It has become a playground of corruption. What started out with good intentions became a road to disaster.

With the demise of the public sector, the only thing left for the world is the personal gain–based private sector. This is not an inspiring prospect. If nothing else, we should remember that greed and corruption are prone to lure each other into solid partnership at the slightest opportunity. Before the world surrenders to greed and corruption, we must seriously examine the strength of social consciousness as a contestant.

■

Critics often argue that micro-credit does not contribute to the economic development of a country. And even if it does contribute something, that something is insignificant.

But it all depends on what one considers economic development. Is it per capita income? Per capita consumption? Per capita anything?

I have always disagreed with this kind of definition of development. I think it misses the essence of development. To me, changing the quality of life of the bottom 50 percent of the population is the essence of development. To be even more rigorous, I would define development by focusing on the quality of life of the lower 25 percent of the population.

This is where growth and development part their ways. Those who believe that growth and development are synonymous, or move at the same speed, assume that the economic layers of society are somehow linked to each other like so many railway carriages, and that one only need stoke the engine for the entire train and everyone in it to move forward at the same speed.

If there is no growth, nothing moves forward—that is true. But the often-used analogy of a train and linked human socioeconomic strata breaks down over one significant factor. A train is drawn by a locomotive located at the front or pushed from behind, or both. But in the case of human society, each economic entity or group has its own engine. Therefore, the combined power of all the engines together pushes and pulls the economy forward. If the society fails to turn on some of the engines, by simply ignoring some of those strata, the combined power of the economy will be much reduced. Worse still, if the engines of the social groups at the tail end are not turned on, those carriages may start sliding backward, independently from the rest of society, and to the detriment of everyone, including those who are better off.

Micro-credit pushes the entire train forward by helping each passenger in the rear (or third-class) carriages. This cannot reduce the speed of the train, it can only increase it, which most of today's so-called development projects fail to do.

Of course, investing in roads, dams, power plants, and airports increases the efficiency of the engines in the first-class carriages. Those are the fanciest and richest ones, and it enhances the train's engine capacity many-fold. But whether these investments can help ignite or enhance the capacity of the engines in the subsequent carriages, in all other layers and strata of society, remains uncertain.

Will micro-credit lead to major infrastructure building? Micro-credit ignites the tiny economic engines of the rejected underclass of society. Once a large number of tiny engines start working, the stage can be set for bigger things.

Microborrowers and microsavers can be organized to own big enterprises, even infrastructure companies. Grameen has created a number of companies for speeding up the process of overcoming poverty. Some of the most exciting of these enterprises are described in the next chapter.

CHAPTER

TWELVE

Beyond Micro-credit:

A New World of

Grameen Enterprises

In 1985, I received a telephone call from the permanent secretary of the Fisheries Ministry of Bangladesh. "Dr. Yunus," said the voice on the other end of the line. "We have not met. But I know you very well through your work. I wanted to discuss a fisheries project with you. Have you ever visited Serajganj?"

"Yes, I have," I answered, "but only in limited areas. We are just expanding our work in Bogra."*

"You must visit the fisheries ministry project in Nimgachi. We have nearly one thousand large ponds that were originally excavated by the Pal kings [local Hindu rulers of the Pal dynasty] over one thousand years ago to provide drinking water for the people and for the king's cattle herds. They have silted up. Our project was supposed to reexcavate them for fish farming."

"What happened to the project?" I asked.

"That's the tragedy. I recently visited the place to find out why the British foreign aid agency refused to give us more money for the project. I was stunned by the blatant corruption and mismanagement. Now I have a request for you."

"What is that?"

---

*Bogra and Serajganj are districts in northern Bangladesh. Nimgachi is an area within Serajganj.

"My request is that you take over the project. You can do whatever you want. We'll stay out of it."

"What am I going to do with hundreds of ponds?"

"Please don't turn down my request. At least make a trip to the project area. You'll be inspired to see the beauty of these ponds and the potential they hold for the country."

"We are a bank. We don't know how to farm fish."

"Yes, I know that. If you think you can't do it, at least take the ponds for safekeeping. The way I see it, if they remain in government hands, nothing will be left of them."

The secretary was both accusing his own staff of corruption and trying to protect the ponds. Though I was reluctant to get involved in something I had no expertise in, I was also tempted by the challenge. I discussed it with my colleagues. They also felt that if the government genuinely wanted to give us the land, we should take it.

A week later I got another telephone call from the secretary, but I did not want to change my position yet, so I told him that my answer was still no.

"I am calling you for another reason," he replied. "I am convening a meeting on the future policy direction of the fisheries ministry. I want you there to help us formulate our ideas."

"If I attend, you'll again bring up the subject of the Nimgachi project and pressure me to take it over," I said.

"I give you my word. I won't bring up the subject of Nimgachi at the meeting."

I laughed and agreed. I laughed because I did not believe that he'd keep his promise. I agreed because I wanted to meet this man who had so much confidence in me, even though we had never met.

There were about a dozen people at the secretariat's meeting. Half of them were top government officials from the fisheries ministry. The other half came from universities and research institutes. The meeting went on for two hours. The secretary did not utter a word about the Nimgachi project.

Just as the meeting was about to conclude, the secretary leaned over and whispered in my ear, "Could you stay for a while so that we can have a cup of tea and a one-on-one discussion?"

When everyone had left, tea and snacks were brought in for us. Grinning at me, the secretary said, "Did you see? I kept my word. I did not bring up the subject of Nimgachi during the meeting. Now that the meeting is over, I am free to bring it up, am I not?"

He narrated the history of the project, the corruption of his staff, his plans about handing the ponds over to Grameen. He said he would be willing to give us the project on our own terms. He then handed me a stack of reports to help me make up my mind.

As I returned to my office, I decided that we should go for it. Here was a most unusual secretary who truly had the good of the country at heart. When the government wants to help the poor it usually comes up with a policy of free distribution—free distribution of money, land, or other assets. But along the way from the government to the poor, the free goods rarely reach the poor as more powerful people line up to take advantage of the distribution system. We wanted to reverse this trend and here was the opportunity. How could I not help the secretary? How could we go wrong in taking over properties from the government?

Fish is an important source of protein for Bengalis, and fishing is a significant income-generating activity. Here was an opportunity to transfer significant assets to the landless poor. The unexcavated ponds could be combined with the untapped abilities of the local poor to create a bold chemistry for improving the quality of their lives. If we succeeded in this venture, we would not only help the locals to feed, clothe, and house themselves but also help them become major economic players. We decided to take on the challenge.

I wrote a long memo to the secretary agreeing to take over the project, but only under certain rigorous conditions. I wanted a ninety-nine–year lease with low annual rent. And I wanted the government to withdraw all its staff as soon as the handing over took place. I also said we required a detailed list of everything that was being granted to us.

I sent the memo and the secretary called me the next day saying that he agreed to all my conditions but that government rules would allow us only a twenty-five–year lease. I replied that that would be acceptable to us. The secretary sounded relieved. It was strange. In my experience with Grameen, I had only met with "Mr. No's" in government offices. Having someone at the highest level of bureaucracy actually seek us out and agree to our conditions was a totally new experience for me.

The secretary moved with lightning speed to get everything done. His proposal went to the president and the land ministry for approval. It was quite a bureaucratic feat, yet the whole thing was achieved within a couple of months.

In January 1986, we signed the agreement with the government regarding the transfer of the Nimgachi project to the Grameen Bank. The project consisted of 783 ponds of various sizes and shapes, with a combined water body of 1,666 acres spread over four subdistricts in Pabna and Serajganj. In 1988, the government leased us more ponds for a total of 808.

We began our adventure in the new world of fisheries with high expectations, but we soon hit rough waters. In 1987, devastating floods hit Bangladesh and caused us serious losses. The following year, we suffered the worst flood in a century. More losses were added. Predator fish remained in the ponds, and our efforts to eradicate them were neutralized by the floods, which brought in new predators.

We inherited so few nurseries and rearing ponds that we had no alternative but to stock our excess hatchlings directly in the ponds. This led to a high mortality rate. The ponds had uneven bottoms, which led to turbidity, high acidity, sedimentation of harmful organic matter, and other problems. And though incidents of theft greatly decreased, poaching persisted, especially in remote areas. We gave up hope for production on the scale we had initially planned.

But more disheartening than the natural disasters was the human resistance to our efforts. From the beginning the old bureaucracy and local vested interests did not accept our presence with grace. The government officials who had been entrusted with the operation of the project were bitter about the decision to let Grameen run their show. They complained that they were being discredited. Their pride was wounded and they felt that Grameen had been brought in to enjoy the fruits of their labor.

Many of these officials also fanned anti-Grameen sentiment among the local people. Local leaders of major political parties were also antagonistic. Leftist leaders argued that development was the job of the government, not of a private bank. But the real source of their anger toward us stemmed from the fact that the politicians were no longer able to exercise influence on the management of the fisheries. In one area, a leading political party organized anti-Grameen demonstrations and public meetings. Leaders tried to convince villagers that we were a foreign organization intent on exploiting the locals and remitting our profits overseas.

The mood of the people ranged from skeptical to openly rebellious. There were days when our staff could not step out of the residential complex for fear of attack. But even during the worst, most tense standoffs, we were confident that we could turn the situation around and win the people's confidence. To that end, we held meetings with the locals and appealed for their support. We promised that proper management of the ponds would benefit not only the landless but the community at large. To prove our good faith, we organized some forty preschool learning centers for poor children. Eventually the patience and sincerity of our staff began to pay off and the initial animosity and suspicion subsided. The ultraleft underground armed revolutionary groups that burned down our offices and forced our staff to leave the villages at gunpoint now disappeared. We could finally concentrate on the production of fish.

The work was difficult. Without first establishing a technical, physical, and managerial base for production and effective control over the ponds, we could not begin to help the local poor. As our staff members had no background in fisheries, we enrolled them in crash courses on fish farming. We sent them to China to learn about pond management and hatchery operations. Eventually our large initial capital investment and staff training began to pay off. We invited the local poor to become our business partners: They contributed their labor and guarded the ponds against poaching while we provided all the technology and management. The harvest was divided on a fifty-fifty basis. Our partners received a good annual income from this agreement. We struggled to cover our costs.

We also adopted a bonus scheme to boost production. If fish from a pond exceeded a predetermined target, the staff was rewarded. The poor, who had stolen fish under the government's management, now became our best farmers, protectors, and partners out of self-interest in their profit share.

In the future, as we overcome our technical, financial, and managerial challenges, we hope to create for-profit subsidiaries of our not-for-profit Fisheries Foundation. The shares in these subsidiaries will be owned by the members of fisheries groups who now participate in the fifty-fifty production partnership. If this model of management and ownership works, we will extend it throughout Bangladesh to revitalize additional idle ponds. If we can combine our micro-credit and pond management programs, we will mobilize two hitherto-underutilized resources that Bangladesh has in abundance: vast numbers of landless poor people and 1.5 million freshwater ponds.

Grameen's experience with fisheries demonstrates that new grassroots systems can be designed and developed from scratch so that the poor can better control sophisticated technology and share in a macroeconomic project. Technology is an essential prerequisite for raising productivity, but it must be directed so that the increased production does not simply end up in the hands of the wealthy.

In Bangladesh, there is no reason why people should remain poor. Our problem is one of management, not lack of resources. With the proper management framework, the rich resources of Bangladesh can solve our poverty problem once and for all.

One such resource is textiles. Bangladesh has a long tradition of making fine hand-woven fabrics such as muslin that for centuries were in demand by the European courts. Unfortunately, with the advent of the industrial revolution in Europe and the sudden boom of machine-made fabrics in England, the demand for Bengali cloth died down. In their enthusiasm to gain control of the market, our colonial masters placed a ban on hand-loom weaving in Bangladesh and even punished those weavers who violated the ban by chopping off their thumbs. Despite such restrictions, hand-loom weavers passed their skill on from generation to generation. When the Indian independence movement began, one of its expressions of rebellion was the boycott of British fabric and the use only of locally produced cloth. Today in Bangladesh, there are 1 million hand-loom weavers desperately looking for a market for their products.

Hand-loom weavers have always been extremely poor. They make beautiful fabrics and manufacture the most gorgeous saris, but their women cannot afford to wear them. Their children go naked. Many of the women who join Grameen come from hand-loom weavers' families. In hand-loom villages we always had repayment problems during a particularly lean month of the year for the hand-loom trade. This lean month lies between two agricultural harvest seasons, when people run out of purchasing power. Grameen's deputy managing director, Khalid Shams, worried greatly about the repayment difficulties of the weaving families. He took great pride in our ancient tradition of weaving, and he wanted to see it regain its rightful place in the economy of Bangladesh.

Khalid wanted to understand the weavers' problems by living with them and experiencing their daily struggle, so he lived for a week in the Grameen branch with the highest density of weavers. He became convinced that the weavers' number one problem was not being able to buy yarn at a fair price. To solve this problem, he met the civil servant in charge of the textile ministry. But, whereas getting permission from the ministry to buy yarn directly from the factory was not difficult, actually receiving the delivery from the factory was quite another matter. We learned the hard way about how the yarn market in Bangladesh works, how textile trade union leaders and a handful of wholesalers control the price and supply of yarn.

Khalid also discovered that Bangladesh was importing roughly $150 million worth of an Indian fabric called Madras Check. We were shocked. While we were trying to create a local market for our own hand-loom fabrics, we were importing $150 million worth of fabric from our neighbor. We were told that the Indian fabric was of a very high quality that could not be matched by our local weavers. But when Khalid circulated some samples from Belkuchi, where some of the best *lunghis* are made, the garment factories and buying houses all agreed that our fabrics were superior to the imported Indian cloth. Still, the buyers did not show any interest in purchasing this local fabric. It was too difficult. They explained that they could not go door to door to each single weaver in Bangladesh to acquire the hundreds of thousands of yards they needed. It was much easier to place a huge order with the Indian suppliers, who could provide them with whatever they needed, right on time.

Khalid tried to interest private businesses in organizing the production and distribution of hand-loom fabrics for the garment industry. As no one showed any interest, Grameen decided to move in by itself. We would play the role of middleman and supplier. We would accept orders from exporters and take responsibility for the quality of the cloth and its delivery. In 1993, we created an independent nonstock, not-for-profit company we called Grameen Uddog ("Grameen Initiatives") to link the traditional hand-loom weavers with the export-oriented garment industry. The weavers, thrilled to participate in the export market, created a beautiful new line of fabrics. We called it Grameen Check.

It was not easy to enter the international marketplace. We had no textile experience. Khalid worked very hard to put together a team and learn the ropes of the business. Grameen is not doing anything fancy—all we do is promote the product, take orders, and work as a marketing agent for independent home-based weavers. We pass on the specifications of the orders to the weavers, give them the best-quality yarn so that they do not wait for working capital, and ensure that they meet the quality controls and deadlines. With our help, weavers do not have to worry about procurement of orders or the marketing of their products. Our method works. During our first year, total sales came to $2.5 million. Three years later, they stood at $15 million. Sales are still growing.

As a product, Grameen Check has great market potential. It is hand woven, 100 percent cotton, and very attractive. In Paris in February 1996, by courtesy of the United Nations Educational, Scientific, and Cultural Organization (UNESCO), we held a fashion show of garments designed and presented by a talented Bangladeshi model, Bibi Russell. Paris fashion personalities, magazines, and other media immediately took up the designs. Today, eight thousand hand-loom weavers produce Grameen Check, which sells in Italy, France, the United Kingdom, and Germany. With all the unemployed weavers in Bangladesh, we could easily raise the production level to 1 million yards per week. We are working to interest more buyers in Europe and North America.

When we were introducing Grameen Check, buyers asked if we could also supply checked flannel. Realizing that we would need our own machines to convert the Grameen Check to Grameen Flannel, we teamed up with a friend of ours, Dr. Zafarullah Chowdhury, who had recently purchased land for a textile factory. This factory, known as Gonoshasthaya Grameen Textile Mills Ltd., went into production in 1998.

Having successfully branched into flannel, we are now trying to produce fabric from jute mixed with cotton. Jute, a natural fiber grown abundantly in Bangladesh, was once used exclusively as a packing material. Grameen is finding new uses for jute by combining it with cotton or silk to make fabrics used in home furnishings. Soon, new technology will provide ways of using jute for clothing at a very competitive price.

Our hope is that as our fabric production becomes more diversified and the market expands, our weavers will revive a beautiful Bengali craft. To this end, we are cooperating with Grameen Foundation USA to open the American market to Grameen textiles. GF-USA is helping us form partnerships with individuals and companies in the United States.

A pleasant surprise during this whole process has been the positive response from the domestic market. All of a sudden, Grameen Check has become a household name and a social statement; to wear Grameen Check indicates pride in Bangladeshi arts and heritage. To cope with this burgeoning domestic market, we created another company, Grameen Shamogree ("Grameen Products"), which focuses its attention on finished goods made from Grameen Check fabrics as well as other Bangladeshi handicrafts.

Khalid was not willing to stop at textiles. His vision for Grameen was far grander. One day in 1994, he introduced me to Iqbal Quadir, a young Bangladeshi American, a graduate of Oberlin College. Khalid said, "Iqbal has an idea. He says we can apply for a license to operate a cellular telephone company in Bangladesh. We can take cellular telephones into the villages."

It sounded like an exciting idea. Step by step, we gathered information on cellular phones. In 1996, the government of Bangladesh issued three cellular licenses, including one to us. We signed the license agreement on November 11, 1996, and I announced to the press that we would launch our service on March 26, 1997, Bangladesh's Independence Day. We formed two independent companies—one for profit (GrameenPhone),* another not for profit (Grameen Telecom).

GrameenPhone received the license. The company is building a nationwide cellular network throughout urban Bangladesh. Grameen Telecom would then buy bulk airtime from GrameenPhone and retail it through Grameen borrowers in rural villages. One Grameen borrower in each of the 68,000 villages would become the "telephone lady" of the village. She sells the service of the telephone to the villagers by operating what we call a "village pay phone." Thus, the village would become connected to the world through one poor woman with access to the most modern communication system available.

As planned, GrameenPhone launched its service on March 26, 1997. The opening ceremony was held at the prime minister's office. Using a Grameen phone, our prime minister, Sheikh Hasina, called the prime minister of Norway, who was enjoying his holiday

---

*GrameenPhone is a consortium made up of four partners: Telenor of Norway (51%), Grameen Telecom (35%), Marubeni of Japan (9.5%), and Gonophone Development Company (4.5%).

in the north of Norway. From our end, the prime minister said, "How's the weather up there?"

"It is very cold here. It is 36°C below zero," answered the Norwegian.

"How can you enjoy yourself in weather like that? You'd better come here for your next holiday. We have a pleasant 32°C in Dhaka."

After this international call, a domestic call came in for our prime minister. It was a Grameen borrower, Laily Begum, from the village of Patira, north of Dhaka, who was calling the prime minister from her cellular phone. Laily Begum was Grameen's first telephone lady, and since then she has earned a substantial income by letting others pay to use her phone.

In 1997, Bangladesh had just about the lowest telephone density in the world: one phone per 300 inhabitants. In a country of 120 million people, we had only 400,000 telephones, and these were all centered in cities, mostly in Dhaka. As many as one-quarter of all phones were out of commission at any given time. With such scarcity, working phones became a symbol of power and authority in Bangladesh. People would wait for years to get a telephone. The more telephones people had on their desk, the more important they were thought to be. A cellular phone was an indicator of great wealth. GrameenPhone now has 850,000 cellular phone subscribers in Bangladesh, of which 24,000 are village phones, operated by the village phone ladies. While the number of village phones is small in relation to the total, the air-time usage on village phones represents 17 percent of total air-time use of GrameenPhone. We now offer the cheapest cellular rate in the world, 9 cents per minute for airtime during peak hours and 6.7 cents per minute during off-peak hours.

One challenge to our cellular phone program is the lack of electricity. Many villages in Bangladesh are not connected to the national grid. To introduce cellular phones to those villages, we are bringing in solar energy. We created Grameen Shakti ("Energy"), a nonprofit company dedicated to developing forms of renewable energy. Grameen Shakti is currently experimenting with solar (photovoltaic) home systems, battery stations, wind turbines, and gasifiers. Gasifiers turn wood or agricultural waste into gas, which is used to generate electricity.

Our phone network has also led us to experiment with the Internet. Grameen Cybernet, an Internet service provider, hopes to create international jobs for the children of Grameen borrowers. These boys and girls will be able to serve companies around the world in various capacities from their own village homes or community office spaces. By bringing Internet facilities into distant rural areas, many labor-intensive enterprises can be located in those otherwise isolated rural areas. These enterprises include data entry services, data management businesses, global answering services, typing services, transcription services, secretarial services, accounting services, and so on.

Finally, a nonprofit Internet service provider, Grameen Communications, will make the Internet available to educational and research institutions in Bangladesh. Many of these institutions do not have reliable telephone lines or the budget to afford Internet facilities. Grameen Communications will offer them packages through which they will solve these problems.

By joining the twentieth century late in the game, Grameen borrowers will benefit from the latest innovations without wasting time or money on the earlier, less efficient and more costly technology. If used properly, technology can help break down structural barriers, distances, and cultural differences. It can introduce rapid social change by linking isolated rural women to friends and distant relatives.

Cynics and critics of our ambitious project claim that high tech will be wasted on the stone age mentality of most of our borrowers. The truth is, we are finding quite the opposite. Without the benefit of a telephone, our villagers waste a lot of time, money, and effort getting messages to dispersed family members. Before, in an emergency situation, if they needed to tell a brother or daughter living in Dhaka to come home, they had to send a messenger in person. That messenger would stop working or studying and take a bus, rickshaw, or train to his or her destination. Measured by this ordeal, the cost of not having access to a phone is obviously quite high.

Another criticism we hear is that the rural poor do not need the luxury of a telephone. But to our telephone lady, the telephone is a very real and practical way to earn money. Besides, a telephone helps Grameen borrowers improve their existing businesses by giving them more information and greater flexibility to buy and sell their products. Without a phone, a borrower who needs to buy raw materials must send a messenger to ask the price and delivery date of her goods. She may have to send her messenger to three or four different suppliers. This can take weeks. With a cellular phone, she can make her calls in the space of half an hour, put in her orders, and immediately increase the profitability of her business.

There is no reason to assume that the Grameen telephone lady will limit herself to renting out her telephone. As technology and energy sources evolve, she may become a sort of one-stop communications center, providing her fellow villagers with fax, e-mail, and ATM capabilities. Today, we are working with high-tech companies in the United States and Europe to develop a prototype of a cyber-kiosk that will allow borrowers to keep abreast of new technologies and to provide these services profitably to the people in their community.

One would think that with all these expansions and modernizations, Grameen had solved many of Bangladesh's fundamental problems. Not true. In Grameen, we have noticed that as borrowers' income increases, they spend more and more on combating malnutrition, diseases, infant and maternal mortality, and other health problems. Given the abominable condition of public health services, our borrowers often give in to the temptation to spend all their new money on traditional healers and sham doctors.

If we could persuade our borrowers to take the money they give to traditional healers and give it instead to a Grameen-sponsored health program, we might provide them with modern and effective health services for almost the same amount of money. That process has begun. We are now trying to make health care available to all members of Grameen families and to all villagers who are not Grameen borrowers on a self-financing, cost recovery basis. We ask our borrowers to pay a fixed amount of three dollars per family per year as a premium to a health insurance program.* Each time they see a doctor, borrowers must pay a nominal amount (less than three cents). Laboratory services and medication are available at a discount. Grameen Health Program is also operating eye camps in the villages, where trained doctors perform, among other services, inter-ocular lens implantation for cataract patients. The cost of the operation is only one thousand taka, which is less than US$20.

During the first three years of operation, the Grameen health program recovered about 60 percent of the cost of providing these medical services. If we can organize a nationwide franchise, we could turn Grameen's health care into a strong, competitive, and sustainable pro-people enterprise.

One reason we are so acutely aware of health problems is that they can destroy even our brightest successes. Morley Safer's *Sixty Minutes* program of 1989 featured one borrower near Chittagong who, thanks to Grameen loans, had risen from being a street beggar to owning seven cows, a large plot of land, a new house, a modern latrine, and a three-wheeled baby taxi for her husband and ensuring a school education for all her children. Morley Safer called her "the picture of contentment and human success," yet when I met her and her husband again in 1996, I could barely recognize them. He had contracted a stomach illness that was never

---

*Non-Grameen borrowers pay a higher fee, the equivalent of five dollars per year, for health coverage for the entire family.

properly diagnosed. To pay for his medical treatment, the couple had sold off their taxi, their land, and their cattle. She was so frail and tired, she did not trust herself to take a new loan. All they had left were four chickens.

I mention this case to indicate how difficult a road we have ahead of us. Grameen is not just a series of success stories. There are constant potholes along the way. Part of our ability to alleviate poverty depends on our willingness to admit failure and to help ensure that the failures do not happen again.

Needless to say, micro-credit cannot solve society's every problem. But it can help to support those who would otherwise fall through the cracks. In our health care expansion, for example, we worried a great deal about how to ensure that Grameen borrowers would build up savings for retirement. We did not want our members to become dependent on their children, the government, Grameen, or businesses that they were no longer able to run. After years of hard work in their micro-businesses, we wanted them to live their final years in dignified retirement. In place of social security, we decided to offer them shares of successful Grameen companies, non-Grameen companies, and Grameen mutual funds. Basically, when a Grameen company such as the Grameen Fisheries Foundation reaches a profitable level, we transform part of it into a for-profit company coowned by Grameen borrowers and the general public through stock options.* In most cases, shares yield dividends and also appreciate in value. To meet a sudden crisis, borrowers may sell some shares for immediate cash. A new Grameen entity called Grameen Securities Management Company facilitates these financial transactions. Interestingly, the Dhaka office of the now-defunct Hong Kong–based investment company Peregrine asked us to merge with it as an alternative to

---

*Alternatively, borrowers can participate in a Grameen-affiliated mutual fund, which may invest part of its assets in such a company.

closing down its Bangladesh operations. We did not go for it, but we interpreted the interest as a powerful statement about the potential strength of our local investment organization. With a base of 2 million families, all involved in micro-business and interested in investing their savings, we have a tremendous untapped market for financial and investment services.

CHAPTER

THIRTEEN

Grameen Bank II

Grameen Bank has come a long way since it began its journey in the village of Jobra in 1976. During this quarter of a century it has faced many operational and organizational problems and gained a lot of experience through its successes and failures. We have gathered many years of experience with the borrowers at our side. Borrowers of Grameen Bank at present own 93 percent of the total equity of the bank; only the remaining 7 percent is owned by the Bangladeshi government. The total number of borrowers is 2.6 million, 95 percent of whom are women.

Grameen Bank has 1,181 branches, works in 42,127 villages, and has a staff of 11,777. The total amount of loans disbursed by Grameen Bank, since inception, is 174.78 billion takas ($3.9 billion). Out of this, 161.33 billion takas ($3.6 billion) has been repaid, with the recovery rate standing at 98 percent.

Grameen is especially proud of its self-reliance. It finances 90 percent of its total outstanding loan of 13.45 billion takas from its own fund and the savings from its depositors, over 82 percent of whom are its own borrowers. Grameen does not anticipate any need to solicit donor money or even take new loans from internal or external sources in the future. In 1995, Grameen decided not to request any more funds from donors. The last installment of donor funds was received in 1998. Grameen's growing amount of deposits should be more than enough to repay its existing loans and run and expand its credit program from now on.

Grameen Bank borrowed 1 billion takas from the Central Bank of Bangladesh and 2 billion takas from commercial banks immediately after the devastating flood of 1998 to give fresh loans to the borrowers, most of whom lost their assets. All these postflood loans have been fully paid off. In addition, it has paid off all other loans that became due so far.

Grameen Bank has made a profit every year since it came into being except in 1983, 1991, and 1992—proving that businesses with social objectives can and do work. (Since the bank's operations began in 1983, it did not make a profit that year. The years 1991 and 1992 were years of massive rehabilitation for Grameen Bank members after a devastating cyclone hit Bangladesh in April 1991. The cyclone killed 150,000 people and affected hundreds of thousands of Grameen borrowers who lost their assets and livelihoods and were unable to pay back their loans on time.) It also publishes its audited balance sheet every year, audited by two Bangladeshi audit firms of international repute.

Grameen Bank provides three types of loans: income-generating loans (with an interest rate of 20 percent), housing loans (with an interest rate of 8 percent), and higher education loans for the children of Grameen families (with an interest rate of 5 percent). All interests are simple interest, calculated on a declining balance method. This means that if a borrower takes a loan of 1,000 takas and pays back the entire amount within a year through weekly installments, she'll pay a total amount of 1,100 takas (i.e., 1,000 takas in principal plus 100 takas as interest for the year).

Grameen believes that education is one of the primary components for moving oneself out of poverty. If current borrowers can educate their families and make their children better prepared to compete in the future, there will be a sustainable improvement for multiple generations. Students who succeed in reaching institutions of higher education are given loans covering tuition, living costs, and other school expenses. So far 466 students have received higher education loans. They are studying at various universities, medical schools, engineering schools, and other professional institutions. Scholarships—with priority given to girls and young women—are earned by the children of Grameen members every year. This encourages them to get better grades in school. An average of 3,700 children at various levels of education receive these scholarships every year. This is a means of in vesting in the future of our members.

■

Grameen Bank launched a program in 2001 to convert its operational methodology into a newer version called the Grameen Generalised System (GGS, or Grameen Bank II). (We now refer to the earlier version as the Grameen Classic System, or GCS.) We sat down in April 2000 to design the new system, part by part, piece by piece. We then test-piloted it immediately in a few branches. We fine-tuned the design, tried again in a larger number of branches, and reworked it. By the beginning of 2001, we had come up with a system that we all liked. All 12,000 staff members participated very actively in designing the product at all stages of its development.

While we were designing and debugging the system, we were deeply concerned about how we would manage the transition from the Grameen Classic System (GCS) to GGS in 41,000 villages without subjecting hundreds of thousands of illiterate borrowers to a large shock and messing up the accounts in 1,175 branches. The transition was very carefully choreographed. We initially put it into action in March 2001. It was a gradual process. By April 2002, two years after we began, Grameen Bank II had emerged. The last branch of Grameen Bank to switch over to Grameen II did so on August 7, 2002. The new Grameen Bank II is now a real functioning institution. This second-generation micro-credit institution appears to be much better equipped than the earlier version.

The central assumption underlying GGS remains the same as it was behind the Grameen Classic System—the firm belief that poor people always pay back their loans. On some occasions they may take longer to pay than originally stipulated, but repay they will. A credit institution dedicated to serving the poor should not get worried the minute a borrower fails to adhere to a strict schedule. Circumstances can befall a poor person over which they have no control. Since the borrower is paying additional interest for the period that she is delayed in repayment, there should be no problem on the institution's part. Micro-credit programs should not fall into the logical trap of conventional banking firms and start looking at their borrowers as some kind of time bombs, ticking away and waiting to create big trouble on prefixed dates.

We wanted to simplify life for our borrowers with GGS. GGS has been built around one prime loan product—called the *basic loan*. The basic loan comes with an exit option. It offers an alternative route to any borrower who needs it, without making her feel guilty about failing to fulfill the requirement of the basic loan. This alternative route is provided through a *flexible loan*.

A flexible loan is simply a rescheduled basic loan, with its own separate set of rules. I have described the basic loan as a "Grameen micro-credit highway." As long as the borrower keeps her schedule, she moves forward uninterrupted, with ease and comfort, on the micro-credit highway. She can pick up speed according to the rules of the highway. If she drives well she can shift to higher and higher gears. In other words, on the Grameen highway, a borrower can routinely upgrade her loan size at each cycle of the loan. This is done on the basis of predetermined rules. She knows ahead of time how much of an enhancement in loan size is coming and can plan her activities accordingly. But if a borrower faces engine trouble (a business slowdown or failure, sickness, family problems, accidents, thefts, natural disaster, etc.) and cannot keep up with the highway speed, she has to quit the highway and take an exit. This detour is called a "flexible loan" or "flexi-loan." It allows her to move at a slower speed more appropriate to her situation. She can reduce the installment size that she can afford to pay by extending the loan period. Taking a detour, however, does not in any way limply that she has changed the objective of her journey. Her immediate goal is to overcome her problems and take as short a detour as possible. A borrower may be lucky and succeed in getting back to the highway (i.e., the basic loan) quickly, or she may have sustained problems and the best she can do is to move from one detour to the next (i.e., moving from one flexi-loan to the next flexi-loan, working out an easier repayment schedule than the previous one), delaying reentry onto the highway. Under the new system, the flexibility is something that the borrower is entitled to, and rescheduling a loan is not seen as an offense or something to be disapproved of. This gives the borrower a dignified way to deal with any problem she may face in repaying her loan.

One big disincentive for a borrower to take the flexi-loan detour is that the moment she exits from the basic loan highway, her loan ceiling (i.e., the maximum amount that she can take out as a loan, built up on the basis of her performance over the years) gets wiped out. When she reenters the highway after completing her detour, her loan ceiling will have to be reconstructed. This will be somewhere between her entry-level loan ceiling and the loan ceiling she enjoyed immediately before taking the detour.

There are many exciting features in GGS, but I think removing tension from micro-credit by allowing the system to be flexible and permanently establishing full dignity to the poor borrowers are the two most important features of them all. Now both sides in the micro-credit system, the lender and the borrowers, can *enjoy* micro-credit, rather than creating occasional nightmares for each other.

■

GGS has also created a methodology that can provide custom-made credit to a poor borrower. GGS allows loans of any duration, such as three, six, or nine months or any number of months and years. GGS allows a staff member to be creative. He can design his loan product to make it the best fit for his client in terms of duration, timing, scheduling the installment, and so on. The more a staff member becomes a creative artist, the better music he can produce. Grameen can identify the levels of creativity among its staff, and GGS allows space for this staff to grow.

■

GGS requires all borrowers with loans above 8,000 takas ($138) to contribute a minimum of 50 takas ($0.86) each month to a pension savings account. After ten years a borrower will receive a guaranteed amount, which is almost double the amount she has put in during those 120 months. This has become an amazingly attractive feature of GGS for the borrowers. Many are coming forward to save more than 50 takas each month. There are borrowers who are saving 500 takas per month. While it has become popular with the borrowers, it is generating a huge cash inflow for the bank. It is now bringing in over 100 million takas ($1.75 million) each month as deposits on pension savings accounts. Grameen Bank can now rest assured that it will have enough of its own money to expand its lending operation in the future. By the same token, branches will now have enough money to carry out their lending programs with their own deposits. All Grameen branches can look forward to becoming self-financed. While the institution moves toward financial self-reliance, the borrowers also move to financial self-reliance as old age approaches. They can have monthly income at retirement out of the accumulated savings in the pension fund. For a poor woman, it is very comforting news.

■

GGS emphasizes receiving deposits from borrowers and non-borrowers. A variety of savings products has been incorporated into the system. The total amount of borrowers' deposits (i.e., savings) today accounts for 70 percent of the total outstanding loans of Grameen Bank. And this is after GB has paid back 3.3 billion takas ($60 million) of its loans to the Central Bank, local commercial banks, and the foreign lenders, which became due for repayment during the past two years.

■

Bangladeshi borrowers always worry what will happen to their debt if they die. Will their family members pay it? They believe that if their debt remains unpaid after their death, their soul cannot rest in peace. Inclusion of a loan insurance program in GGS has made them very happy. The insurance program is extremely simple. On the last day of every year, the borrower is required to put a small amount of money in a loan insurance savings account. It is calculated on the basis of the outstanding loan and interest of the borrower on that day. She deposits 2.5 percent of the outstanding amount. If a borrower dies any time during the next year, her entire outstanding amount is covered by the insurance fund. This money is provided by the interest income of the loan insurance savings account. In addition, her family receives back the amount she saved in the loan insurance savings account. Borrowers find it unbelievably generous. Everybody loves it.

Total deposits under loan insurance savings now stand at 321.55 million takas ($5.55 million). Since this insurance program was introduced in 2001 under Grameen Bank II, 4,215 borrowers have died, and total outstanding loans and interest of 25.99 million takas left to be repaid was covered by the bank under this plan. Each year, families of deceased borrowers of Grameen Bank receive a total of 8–10 million takas in loan insurance benefits. Each family receives up to a maximum of 2,000 takas. A total of 61,653 Grameen borrowers have died since 1983. Their families collectively received a total amount of 124.86 million takas ($3.04 million). Borrowers are not required to pay any premium for this insurance. Borrowers receive this insurance coverage simply by being a shareholder of the bank.

■

I have never seen Grameen staff charged with so much enthusiasm and energy than after the introduction of GGS. They were all captivated by the idea of creating Grameen Bank II. The staff's energy level is now at its peak. Every time one talks to staff members they appear as if they are having the most fun of their lives working for Grameen. You just can't stop them.

Creating Five Star branches really caught their imagination. Grameen Bank provides color-coded stars to branches for 100 percent achievement of a specific task. Five stars indicate a branch has reached the highest level of performance. At the end of 2002, branches showed the followed results:

- 696 branches, out of the total of 1,178 branches, received green stars for maintaining a 100 percent repayment record.

- 437 branches received blue stars for earning a profit. (Grameen Bank as a whole earns a profit because of the revenue it generates from the interest payments made by the branches on the funds borrowed from the head office.)

- 213 branches earned violet stars by generating a surplus of deposits over the loans outstanding in those branches. These branches not only carry out their business with their own funds, but also contribute their surpluses to meet the fund requirement of deficit branches.

- 61 branches have applied for brown stars for ensuring an education for 100 percent of the children of their Grameen families. After the completion of the verification process, their stars will be confirmed.

- 21 branches applied for red stars, indicating that they have succeeded in taking 100 percent of their borrowers' families over the poverty line. The star will be confirmed only after the verification procedure is completed.

- 772 branches (i.e., two-thirds of all branches) received a total of 1,346 stars, an average of 1.74 stars per branch.

Each month branches are coming closer to achieving new stars. Grameen staff members look forward to transforming all the branches of Grameen Bank into Five Star branches. Each staff member can earn stars, even when the branch has yet to receive any stars, by simply fulfilling the same conditions for the centers for which he is responsible.

Grameen staff members proudly display their stars on formal occasions. It has generated a burst of energy all around. They are not doing it for any monetary benefit. They are doing it in the spirit of competition—to be ahead of their peers; to create a record for their branches, areas, or zones; to make a personal contribution in changing the economic and social conditions of the poor families they are working for and, above all, to prove their worth to themselves. Observing this phenomenon, one cannot but wonder how an environment can make people despair and sit idle and then, by changing the conditions, one can transform the same people into matchless performers.

Grameen Bank II has defined micro-credit in very simple terms. It has provided a powerful methodology to achieve its mission. Coming years will show what impact it makes in the lives of the poor in Bangladesh and globally. It has already proven to be a wonderful and exciting experience for Grameen staff members and the borrowers. It has raised our work to a new level of efficiency and effectiveness.

CHAPTER

FOURTEEN

The Future

We often refer to the "next century" as if we were talking about the next twenty-four hours. But the next century means the next 100 years—and we are already on our way. I don't think anybody has the knowledge or wisdom to predict what will happen to the world and its inhabitants during the next 100 years. The world is changing in such unpredictable ways and will continue to become more and more unpredictable as we move through this century. All we can say with a fair amount of certainty is that the speed of change will become faster and faster—it is very unlikely to slow down. Take all the accumulated knowledge, discoveries, and inventions up until the end of the twentieth century, and in the next fifty years alone, this will grow perhaps several times. That is the kind of incredible speed of change that we are approaching.

If somehow we could come back to today's world 100 years from now, we would definitely feel as if we were visitors from some prehistoric age. If we try to imagine what the world will be like twenty-five years from today, we would have to create science fiction.

The momentum for change is clearly in place. The insatiable quest for knowing the unknown, the eagerness of business to put technology at the service of consumers, and the military arms race between nations have all helped create this momentum. The real question is whether these changes will bring the human race closer to or farther away from desirable social and economic conditions.

The answer is obvious. If we consider ourselves passengers on "Spaceship Earth," we will find ourselves on a pilotless journey with no discernable route to follow. If we can convince ourselves that we are actually the crew of this spaceship, and that we must reach a specific socioeconomic destination, then we will continue to approach that destination—even if we make mistakes or take detours along the way.

We need to know the destination—if not in a precise way, then at least a generalized way. Before we actually translate something into reality, we must be able to dream about it. Any socioeconomic dream is nothing but the first step in the process of mapping the course to our destination. If we do a good job in identifying our destination, more innovations and changes will take place to help us reach it.

So the real question is not so much where *we* will be in the year 2050, but where we would like *the world* to be in 2050.

By that time, I want to see a world free from poverty. This means that there will not be a single human being on this planet that may be described as a poor person or who is unable to meet his or her basic needs. By then, the word "poverty" will no longer have relevance. It will be understood only with reference to the past.

Poverty does not belong in civilized human society. Its proper place is in a museum. That's where it will be. When schoolchildren go with their teachers and tour the poverty museums, they will be horrified to see the misery and indignity of human beings. They will blame their forefathers for tolerating this inhumane condition and for allowing it to continue in such a large segment of the population until the early part of the twenty-first century.

I have always believed that the elimination of poverty from the world is a matter of will. Even today we don't pay serious attention to the issue of poverty, because the powerful remain relatively untouched by it. Most people distance themselves from the issue by saying that if the poor worked harder, they wouldn't be poor.

When we want to help the poor, we usually offer them charity. Most often we use charity to avoid recognizing the problem and finding a solution for it. Charity becomes a way to shrug off our responsibility. But charity is no solution to poverty. Charity only perpetuates poverty by taking the initiative away from the poor. Charity allows us to go ahead with our own lives without worrying about the lives of the poor. Charity appeases our consciences.

The real issue is creating a level playing field for everybody—rich and poor countries, powerful and small enterprises—giving every human being a fair chance. As globalization continues to encroach on our socioeconomic realities, the creation of this level playing field can become seriously endangered unless we initiate a global debate and generally agree on the features of a "right" architecture of globalization, rather than drift into something terribly wrong in the absence of a framework for action. This framework will no doubt have many features, but we can keep in mind the following: The rule of "strongest takes it all" must be replaced by a rule that ensures everybody a place and a piece of the action. "Free trade" must mean freedom for the weakest. The poor must be made active players, rather than passive victims, in the process of globalization. Globalization must promote harmony and partnership between the big and the small economies, rather than become a vehicle for unhindered takeovers by the rich economies. Globalization must ensure the easiest movement of people across borders. Each nation, especially poor ones, must make serious and continuous efforts to bring information technology to the poor people to enable them to take maximum advantage of globalization. Social entrepreneurs must be supported and encouraged to get involved in the process of globalization to make it friendly to the poor. Special privileges should be offered to them to let them scale up and multiply.

Human society has tried in many ways to ensure equality of opportunity, but poverty remains. We expect the state to take care of the poor and have wound up with massive bureaucracies to look after the poor. A large amount of taxpayers' money is set aside to finance the programs administered by these bureaucracies. But whatever governmental programs have achieved, they certainly have not created equality of opportunity. Poverty is very often handed down from one generation to the next.

As we proceed through the early days of this new millenium, it would serve us well to strive toward the daring Millennium Development Goals set by the Millennium Summit of world leaders at the United Nations in June 2000. The most daring of these goals is an entirely achievable one: halving poverty by 2015. I am totally convinced from my experience of working with poor people that they can get themselves out of poverty if we give them the same or similar opportunities as we give to others. The poor themselves can create a poverty-free world. All we have to do is to free them from the chains that we have put around them.

In order to reduce, and ultimately eliminate, poverty, we must go back to the drawing board. Concepts, institutions, and analytical frames—the conditions that created poverty—cannot end poverty. If we can intelligently rework the frame conditions, then poverty will be gone, never to come back again. We must widen our concept of employment, ensure financial services even to the poorest person, and recognize every single human being as a potential entrepreneur.

Changes are products of intensive effort. The intensity of effort depends on the felt need for change and the resources that are mobilized to bring about the changes desired. In a greed-based economy, obviously, changes will be greed-driven. These changes may not always be socially desirable. Socially desired changes may not be attractive from the greed perspective.

That is why socially conscious organizations are needed, and the state and civil society should provide financial and other resources to them. Such organizations will continually devote their attention and research and development money to those areas of innovation, adaptation, and development in technology that will facilitate the achievement of beneficial social goals. They will also monitor the greed-driven developments in technology to ensure that such technologies do not lead societies in undesirable directions.

I believe that one of the best ways forward is to encourage social entrepreneurs. The behavior patterns of a social-objective–driven entrepreneur, i.e., a social entrepreneur, are as follows:

- He (or she) competes in the marketplace with all other competitors but is inspired by a set of social objectives. This is the basic reason for being in the business.

- He may earn personal profit as well. This personal profit may range from zero to a significantly large amount, even larger than his personal-gain–driven competitor. But in his case, personal profit is a secondary consideration, rather than the prime consideration. On the other hand a personal-profit–driven entrepreneur may contribute in achieving some social objectives. But this will be a by-product of his business, or a secondary consideration. This will not make him a social entrepreneur.

- The higher the social impact per dollar invested, the higher the market rating of the social entrepreneur. Here, the "market" will consist of potential investors who are looking for opportunities to invest their money in social-objective–driven enterprises. Social-investment dollars will move from low social impact enterprises to higher impact enterprises, from general impact enterprises to specific and visible impact enterprises, from traditional social enterprises to highly innovative and efficient enterprises.

Social-objective–driven investors will need a separate (i.e., social) stock market, as well as separate rating agencies, financial institutions, mutual funds, venture capital, and so on. Almost everything that we have for profit-driven enterprises will be needed for social-objective–driven enterprises—such as audit firms, due diligence and impact assessment methodologies, regulatory framework, standardization, and the like—only in a different context and with different methodologies.

Because of the way in which the orthodoxy of economics has given shape to the existing world, all the investment money now is locked up in only one category of investment: investment for making personal profit. This has happened because people have not been offered any choice. There is only one type of competition: competition to amass more personal wealth. The moment we open the door to making a social impact through investments, investors will start putting their investment dollars through this door as well. Initially, some investors will divert only a part, and maybe a small part, of their investment money to social enterprises. But if social entrepreneurs show concrete impact, then this flow will become larger and larger. Soon, a new type of investor will begin appearing on the scene—those who will put all or almost all their investment money into social investments.

Some of the existing profit-driven entrepreneurs may start revealing another dimension of their entrepreneurial ability. They may successfully operate in both the worlds: as conventional profit-seekers in one, as dedicated social entrepreneurs in another.

If the social enterprises can demonstrate high impact and creative enterprise designs, a day may come when personal profit–driven enterprises will find themselves hard-pressed to protect their market share. They'll be forced to imitate the language and style of social enterprises to stay in business.

If socially motivated people can dedicate their lives in politics to bring change in their communities, nations, and to the world, I see no reason why some socially motivated people will not dedicate their lives to building and operating social-objective– driven enterprises. So far they have not done so, because neither the opportunity nor the supportive framework exist. We must change this situation.

A completely new world can be created by making space for the social entrepreneurs and the social investors in the business world. This is a very important agenda for all of us. Eliminating poverty will become so much easier if social entrepreneurs can take up the challenge of ending poverty and if social investors can use their investment money to support the work of social entrepreneurs.

As recent developments show, there is one particular technology that is going to change the world in the immediate future far more rapidly and fundamentally than any other technology in human history. This may be broadly described as *information and communication technology*. Already, its rate of expansion is phenomenal.

Take the Internet, for example. It is spreading at an exponential rate. At its present rate of expansion, Internet use worldwide is doubling every year. The most attractive aspect of this spread of information and communications technology is that it is not under anyone's control. Neither government, nor big business, nor anyone of any authority can restrict the flow of information through the Internet. And it is becoming cheaper every day.

Information and communication technology gives us reason to hope that we are approaching a world free of power brokers and knowledge brokers. Individuals will be in command. There will be no screening authority on center stage. This is particularly exciting for all disadvantaged groups, voiceless groups, and minority groups. Any power built on exclusive access to information will disintegrate. Every common citizen will have almost as much access to information as the head of a government. Leadership will have to be based on vision and integrity, rather than on the manipulation of information.

What direction would I like to see this information and communication technology take? I would like to see that all information be available to all people (including the poorest, the most ignorant, and the most powerless) at all times, almost cost-free, irrespective of distance. Communication between any two persons anywhere in the world should be as easy as talking to your best friend while sitting together on a park bench. All academic and social institutions should be turned into nodal points for the dissemination of information.

Access to information is empowering: GrameenPhone brings Internet–enabled mobile phones to the Grameen borrowers and makes them "telephone ladies" of the villages. By March 2003, there were more than 25,000 telephone ladies selling telephone services in half the villages of Bangladesh. Many of these phones are solar-powered, because electricity does not exist in those villages. Soon these women can become "Internet ladies" if we can design the appropriate services for them. The technology is already in their hands: Families in remote villages of Bangladesh are able to communicate with relatives in distant parts of the world, conduct business, and lead more informed lives. While extending telecommunications services to the poor, GrameenPhone has also done very well as a business. It has expanded its services to become the largest mobile-phone company in South Asia in its five years of operation.

At each step, future information and communication technology should be creating a global environment to unleash the creativity, ingenuity, and productivity in every human being. Any person anywhere should be able to enroll in any academic institution on the basis of his or her interest and ability, irrespective of his or her social upbringing, geographic location, or financial capacity.

The entire concept of an academic institution would also be vastly different from what it is today. In such an environment, it would not be surprising to learn that the most creative student in a very prestigious university comes from a poor family in a remote village in China, or Ethiopia, or Bangladesh—and that she or he has never yet visited a town.

Another "access" I would like to see is access to the market: I would like to see all barriers and protections around world markets disappear. Protectionism is built up in each nation in the name of the poor, but its real beneficiaries are the rich and clever people who know how to manipulate the system. By contrast, the poor have a better chance in a bigger open market than in a smaller protected market. Everyone would benefit from the free flow of commodities, finances, and people.

It does not make sense to build high walls around the borders of our countries. Passports and visas are a twentieth-century phenomenon that did not really exist before that. Let us leave them behind with the century that invented them. Let us take pride in our human identity above all other identities. Let us wave our national flags, celebrate our regional, national, racial, local, religious, political, and cultural identities, but not by offending others, not by claiming supremacy. Instead, we should glorify in the unity of humankind, strengthened and enhanced through the friendly competition of cultures, religions, and other diversities.

Needless to say, technology as well as economic necessity is bringing us closer to this borderless, distanceless world. Let us welcome it with applause.

Europe is now leading the way in creating a free and open market among nations. Other regional associations and groupings of countries can follow Europe's initiative. Later we can move from regional to interregional, and finally to the free global movement of people, finance, commodities, and services from any one location in the world to any other. With the concept of national government waiting to be drastically redefined in the context of new economic and technological realities, it would be a natural step to go beyond political borders to seek friends and partners without state authority intervening in such matters.

My close friend Sam Daley-Harris, the executive director of RESULTS, was getting tired of lobbying the U.S. Congress for tiny sums of money. He could see that despite his great work in alleviating poverty, the problem was simply too big. Something dramatic was needed. Sam had witnessed the amazing success of Jim Grant, the executive director of the United Nations Children's

Fund (UNICEF), and his Children's Summit of 1990, when the world's leaders came to New York City and signed on to ambitious goals. So Sam started toying with the idea of a gala event, a summit for micro-credit. He sought a reasonable but ambitious target for the summit. With John Hatch of the Foundation for International Community Assistance (FINCA), he articulated his new vision: to reach the 200 million poorest families—the entire population of poor people in the world—through micro-credit within ten years.

I did not think that Sam's goal was feasible. To be taken seriously, we needed a more reasonable goal. I suggested we aim to reach the 100 million poorest families in the coming ten years (at that time, 1996–2005). Agreeing with my revised figure as our official goal, Sam proposed that we organize a world summit.

Drafting our declaration proved to be very contentious. Everyone wanted to rewrite the declaration, and I was disappointed to see how the summit preparations opened up conflicts among various organizations—all of which were trying to achieve the same thing: poverty alleviation. Sam grew increasingly frustrated. I tried to cheer him up by saying that we had to confront all our academic, institutional, and philosophical differences head-on. It was easy for me to say this from the safety of Dhaka, but Sam was the focal point for everyone's anger.

Summit preparations were hectic, but the outpouring of support thrilled us. Held February 2–4, 1997, the Microcredit Summit certainly succeeded in mobilizing worldwide action. About 3,000 people from 137 countries gathered in Washington, D.C. The three cochairs of the summit, First Lady Hillary Rodham Clinton, Queen Sofia of Spain, and Tsutomu Hata, the former prime minister of Japan, made passionate and forceful speeches. Hillary Clinton hailed the summit as "one of the most important gatherings that we could have anywhere in our world." She went on to explain:

It [micro-credit] is not just about giving individuals economic opportunity. It is about community. It is about responsibility. It is about seeing how we are all interconnected and interdependent in today's world. It is recognizing that in our country, the fate of welfare recipients in Denver or Washington is inextricably bound up with all of ours. It is understanding how lifting people out of poverty in India or Bangladesh rebounds to the benefit of the entire community and creates fertile ground for democracy to live and grow, because people have hope in the future.

Sheikh Hasina, the prime minister of Bangladesh, chaired the summit's operating plenary session. On the podium she was joined by Alpha Oumar Konare, the president of Mali; Y. K. Museveni, the president of Uganda; P. M. Mocumbi, the prime minister of Mozambique; Alberto Fujimori, the president of Peru; Queen Sofia of Spain; Tsutomu Hata; Siti Hasmah, the First Lady of Malaysia; and myself. It was an electrifying start to an historic event.

The Summit organized the participants into separate specialized councils: the Council of Practitioners, the Council of Donor Agencies, the Council of Corporations, the Council of Religious Institutions, the Council of UN Agencies, the Council of International Financial Institutions, the Council of Advocates, the Council of NGOs, and the Council of Parliamentarians.

It was indeed a macroevent for micro-credit. During those three days, the whole world came together to discuss solutions to poverty. And the energy generated by listening to other leaders and other advocates, and by meeting so many colleagues, friends, and supporters, brought tears to our eyes. It was obvious to all of us that if we could maintain this level of interest during the subsequent nine years, we could not only meet but overshoot the stated goal of the summit.

Robert Rubin, the secretary of the U.S. Treasury; Jim Wolfensohn, the president of the World Bank; Gus Speth, the administrator of the United Nations Development Program (UNDP); Carol Bellamy, the executive director of UNICEF; Dr. Nafis Sadik, the executive director of the United Nations Fund for Population Activities (UNFPA); Federico Mayor, the secretary-general of UNESCO; Huguette Labelle, the president of the International Development Agency; Brian Atwood, the administrator of USAID; and Fawzi al-Sultan, the president of IFAD, all proved to be inspiring speakers at the plenary sessions. Each one declared his or her uncompromising commitment to the alleviation and eradication of poverty through micro-credit.

The late Bella Abzug, cochair of the Council of Advocates, brought the delegates to their feet when she said, "Never, never, never underestimate the historic importance of what we do here today. And no matter how steep the pass, how discouraging the pace, I ask you to never give in and never give up." The delegates made their response very clear by thumping their applause.

When my turn came to speak at the operating plenary session of the summit, I found myself thinking of Jobra and my very first borrowers—those who were raised to think that they were nobodies, worth nothing, and who had become sudden heroes at this summit. It was those people, with their lives of simple dignity, who had radically changed me from a bird's-eye–view economist, teaching elegant theories in a classroom, to a worm's-eye–view practitioner, helping to introduce real and lasting change into people's lives. I sensed that here, in this hotel ballroom in Washington, D.C., we had enough political leadership to make things really change on a global level. At last we could reach the millions of poor in the world who were waiting for us to help them become self-sufficient.

I stood up and made the following statement:

As we assemble here, I ask myself, "What is the Microcredit Summit about? Is it just another Washington gala event?" To me, this summit is a grand celebration. We are celebrating the freeing of credit from the bondage of collateral. This summit pronounces the end of a long era of financial apartheid. This summit declares that credit is more than business. Like food, credit is a human right.

This summit is about setting the stage to unleash the human creativity and potential of the poor. This summit is to guarantee every poor person the chance to undertake responsibility and to reclaim his or her own human dignity.

This summit is to celebrate the success of millions of determined women who have transformed their lives from extreme poverty to dignified self-sufficiency through micro-credit programs.

This summit is not a fund-raising event. I repeat: This summit wants to inspire the world by putting together all the good news we have created during the past years. This summit wants to build will, wants to build capacity, wants to end poverty in the world.

Only one hundred years ago, men were still struggling to find a way to fly. Many people doubted them and looked upon them as crazy people. But in 1903, the Wright brothers flew their first plane. It stayed in the air for just twelve seconds. It traveled only 120 feet. At that moment the seed of a new world was planted. Only sixty-five years later, man confidently traveled to the moon, gathered up moon rocks, and returned to Earth. The whole world watched every moment of it on television.

In the micro-credit field, we are just testing our wings in a Wright brother's plane. We are covering 120 feet here, 500 feet there. Some find our plane unsafe, some find it clumsy, some find it unfit for the job. We can assure you we'll be ready with our booster rockets.

We believe that poverty does not belong in a civilized human society. It belongs in museums. This summit is about creating a process, which will send poverty to the museum.

Only sixty-five years after the twelve-second flight of the Wright brothers, man went to the moon. Sixty-five years after this summit, we will also go to our moon. We will create a poverty-free world.

With the energy that I feel in this room, I am more confident than ever before that we'll make it. Ladies and gentlemen, let us make it! Thank you.

As I finished my statement, I looked at the audience. I knew there was applause, but I did not hear it. I was trying to imagine a world without poverty. Could anyone really conceive of such a world? What would it be like? Would it really work?

■

The Microcredit Summit of 1997 set the goal to reach the world's 100 million poorest families with micro-credit, along with other financial services, preferably through the women in those families by 2005. During the Microcredit Summit +5, held in New York City in November 2002, we reviewed the progress made during the last five years toward achieving this goal. Figures compiled by the Microcredit Summit Campaign show that by the end of 2001 more that 54 million families around the world benefited from micro-credit. Of this number, 26.8 million are among the poorest, or those who live with less than $1 a day. This is impressive progress from 1997, when we could count only 7.6 million poorest families helped.

I am guessing that by the end of 2002 we'll have reached at least 35 million poorest families with micro-credit. If this turns out to be close to the real figure this would be significant progress. This would mean that we have crossed over a quarter of the path by 2001 and over a third of the path by 2002, and most likely we'll cross the halfway mark, or 50 million families, by 2003. Once we cross the halfway mark, we'll be better equipped psychologically and institutionally to cover the remaining half of the long journey. If this works out, it will mean that we have a good chance to make it to 100 million, or reasonably close to it, by 2005.

■

To me, a world without poverty means a world in which every person can take care of his or her basic life needs. In such a world, nobody would die of hunger or suffer from malnutrition. This is a goal world leaders have been calling for for decades, but they have never set out any way of achieving it.

Each day, some 35,000 children around the world die from hunger-related diseases. In a poverty-free world, no children would die of such causes. All people would have access to education and health-care services because they would be able to afford them. All state organizations that provide free or subsidized services for the poor could be done away with. There would be no need for welfare agencies, handouts, soup kitchens, food stamps, free schools, free hospital care. There would be no begging in the streets. State-run safety-net programs would have no rationale to exist. State–run social security programs and income-support programs would be unnecessary. Social structures in a poverty-free world would, of course, be quite different from those that exist today. But nobody would be at the mercy of anyone else, and that is what would make all the difference between a world without poverty and one riddled with it.

Finally, a poverty-free world would be economically much stronger and far more stable than the world is today.

The 20 percent of the world's inhabitants who currently live a life of extreme poverty would become income earners and income spenders. They would generate extra demand in the market, spurring growth in the world economy. They would bring their creativity and innovations into the marketplace to increase the world's productive capacity. And because people would become poor on a temporary and limited basis, the economy would probably not go through extreme swings. We would avoid boom-and-bust cycles and be able to surmount man-made disasters with greater ease.

But even in a poverty-free world where all people would earn enough to care for themselves and their families, there would still be situations of temporary poverty due to sudden catastrophes or unforeseeable misfortunes, bankruptcy, business downturns, disease, or other disasters.

A poverty-free world might see groups of people or entire regions devastated by some shared disaster, such as floods, fire, cyclones, riots, or earthquakes. But such temporary problems could be taken care of by market mechanisms through insurance and other self-paying programs—assisted, of course, by social-consciousness–driven enterprises.

There will always be differences in lifestyle between people at the bottom of society and those at the top income levels. But those differences will exist only between the middle class and the luxury class, not the third and fourth classes of the current system.

Can we really create a poverty-free world? A world without third-class or fourth-class citizens, a world without a hungry, illiterate, barefoot, underclass? Yes we can, in the same way we can create sovereign states, or democratic political systems, or free-market economies. A poverty-free world might not be perfect, but it would be the best approximation of the ideal.

We have created a slavery-free world, a smallpox-free world, an apartheid-free world. Creating a poverty-free world would be greater than all these accomplishments while at the same time reinforcing them. This would be a world that we could all be proud to live in.

A PREVIEW OF
CREATING A WORLD WITHOUT POVERTY

The Next Big Idea

For thirty-one years, I've been working with poor people, particularly the poor women of Bangladesh, trying to do the best I could to change their lives. Much of that work was through Grameen Bank, through microcredit, which has become known around the world.

It was my experience with microcredit and with Grameen bank that led me to another idea, one I have been developing for some years now. Seeing that many poor people remain poor, I came to realize that one particular problem lay in our conceptual framework. That led me to address the issue of business.

Today, when we think of business we think of enterprises that are dedicated to making money—to profit maximization. To me, that's too narrow a definition of people as economic participants. Human beings are much more complex than just being instruments for making money. So I began to imagine another dimension—a dimension where human beings want to be of help to other people, to create a new kind of world through economic activity. This requires a new kind of business—one that I call a *social business.*

A social business is a non-loss, non-dividend enterprise, created with the intention to do good to people, to bring positive changes to the world, without any short-term expectation of making money out of it. That is the subject of my new book, *Creating a World Without Poverty*. It describes how social business can change the world and end poverty on this planet.

There I'll be describing what social business is all about, how it can be created, how it fits into all our desires and wishes. This is not something I've had to invent: It's inherent in people, it simply it never had the occasion to release itself. So I'm just describing a framework in which people can express themselves, by creating social businesses, to address such issues as poverty, child labor, homelessness, the environment—anything we see that needs to be changed in order to have a better world. We don't have to put everything on the shoulders of the government. Governments are limited; they cannot do everything, and we have responsibilities as citizens. Social business is one way we can address them.

To free-market fundamentalists, social business might seem blasphemous. The idea of a business with objectives other than profit has no place in their existing theology of capitalism. Yet surely no harm will be done to the free market if not all businesses are profit maximizing businesses (PMBs). Surely capitalism is amenable to improvements. And surely the stakes are too high to go on the way we have been going. By insisting that all businesses, by definition, must necessarily be PMBs and by treating this as some kind of axiomatic truth, we have created a world that ignores the multi-dimensional nature of human beings. As a result, businesses remain incapable of addressing many of our most pressing social problems.

We need to recognize the real human being and his or her multifaceted desires. In order to do that, we need a new type of business that pursues goals other than making personal profit—a business that is totally dedicated to solving social and environmental problems.

In its organizational structure, this new business is basically the same as the existing PMB. But it differs in its objectives. Like other businesses, it employs workers, creates goods or services, and provides these to customers for a price consistent with its objective. But its underlying objective—and the criterion by which it should be evaluated—is to create social benefits for those whose lives it touches. The company itself may earn a profit, but the investors who support it do not take any profits out of the company, except recouping an amount equivalent to their original investment, over a period of time. A social business is a company that is cause-driven rather than profit-driven, with the potential to act as a change agent for the world.

A social business is not a charity. It is a business in every sense. It has to recover its full costs while achieving its social objective. When you are running a business, you think differently and work differently than when you are running a charity. And this makes all the difference in defining social business and its impact on society.

There are many organizations in the world today that concentrate on creating social benefit. Most do *not* recover their total costs. Nonprofit organizations and nongovernmental organizations rely on charitable donations, foundation grants, or government support to implement their programs. Most of their leaders are dedicated people doing commendable work, but since they do not recover their costs from their operations, they are forced to devote part of their time and energy, sometimes a significant part, to raising money.

A social business is different. Operated in accordance with management principles just like a traditional PMB, a social business aims for full cost recovery, and more, even as it concentrates on creating products or services that provide a social benefit. It pursues this goal by charging a price or fee for the products or services it creates.

How can the products or services sold by a social business provide a social benefit? There are countless ways. For a few examples, imagine:

- A social business that manufactures and sells high-quality, nutritious food products at very low prices to a targeted market of poor and underfed children. These products can be cheaper because they do not compete in the luxury market and therefore don't require costly packaging or advertising, besides not being under compulsion to maximize profit.

- A social business that designs and markets health insurance policies that provide affordable medical care to the poor.

- A social business that develops renewable-energy systems and sells them at reasonable prices to rural communities that otherwise can't afford access to energy.

- A social business that recycles garbage, sewage, and other waste products that would otherwise generate pollution in poor or politically powerless neighborhoods.

In each of these cases, and in the many other kinds of social businesses that could be imagined, the company is providing a product or service that generates sales revenue even as it benefits the poor or society at large.

A social-objective-driven project that charges a price or fee for its products or services but cannot cover its costs fully does not qualify as a social business. As long as it has to rely on subsidies and donations to cover its losses, such an organization remains in the category of a charity. But once such a project achieves full cost recovery, on a sustained basis, it graduates into another world— the world of business. Only then can it be called a social business.

The achievement of full cost recovery is a moment worth celebrating. Once a social-objective-driven project overcomes the gravitational force of financial dependence, it is ready for space flight. Such a project is self-sustaining and enjoys the potential for almost unlimited growth and expansion. And as the social business grows, so do the benefits it provides to society.

Thus, a social business is designed and operated as a business enterprise, with products, services, customers, markets, expenses, and revenues—but with the profit-maximization principle replaced by the social-benefit principle. Rather than seeking to amass the highest possible level of financial profit to be enjoyed by the investors, the social business seeks to achieve a social objective.

Social Business Profits Stay Within the Business

A social business differs from a charity or an NGO or a nonprofit group in another important way. Unlike those organizations, but like a traditional PMB, a social business has owners who are entitled to recoup their investments. It may be owned by one or more individuals, either as a sole proprietorship or a partnership, or by one or more investors, who pool their money to fund the social business and hire professional managers to run it. It may be also owned by a government or a charity, or any combination of different kinds of owners.

Like any business, a social business cannot incur losses indefinitely. But any profit it earns does not go to those who invest in it. Thus, a social business might be defined as a *non-loss, non-dividend business.* Rather than being passed on to investors, the surplus generated by the social business is reinvested in the business. Ultimately, it is passed on to the target group of beneficiaries in such forms as lower prices, better service, and greater accessibility.

Profitability is important to a social business. Wherever possible, without compromising the social objective, social businesses should make profit for two reasons: First, to pay back investors; and second, to support the pursuit of long-term social goals.

Like a traditional PMB, a social business needs to have a long-term road map. Generating a surplus enables the social business to expand its horizons in many ways—by moving into new geographic areas, improving the range or quality of goods or services offered, mounting research and development efforts, increasing process efficiencies, introducing new technologies, or making innovations in marketing or service delivery so as to reach deeper layers of low-income people.

However, the bottom line for the social business is to operate without incurring losses while serving the people and the planet—and in particular those among us who are most disadvantaged—in the best possible manner.

How long will it take for investors to get back their investment in a social business? That is up to the management of the social business and the investors themselves. The proposed payback period would be specified in the investment prospectus: It might be five years, or ten, or twenty. Investors could choose the appropriate social business in which to invest partly on the basis of this time frame and on their own anticipated needs, as well as their preference for a particular social objective.

Once the initial investment funds are recouped, investors can decide what to do with those funds. They might reinvest in the same social business, invest in another social business or a PMB, or use the money for personal purposes. In any case, they remain as much owners of the social business as before, and have as much control over the company as before.

Why would investors put their money into a social business? Generally speaking, people will invest in a social business for the same kind of personal satisfaction that they can get from philanthropy. The satisfaction may be even greater, since the company they have created will continue to work for the intended social benefit for more and more people without ever stopping. The many billions of dollars that people around the world donate to charitable causes every year demonstrate that they have a hunger to give money in a way that will benefit other human beings. But investing in a social business has several enormous differences from philanthropy.

First, the business one creates with social business is self-sustaining. There is no need to pump in money every year. It is self-propelling, self-perpetuating, and self-expanding. Once it is set up, it continues to grow on its own. You get more social benefits for your money.

Second, investors in a social business get their money back. They can reinvest in the same or a different social business. This way, the same money can bring more social benefits.

Since it is business, businesspeople will find this as an exciting opportunity to not only bring money to social business but to leverage their own business skill and creativity to solve social problems. Not only does the investor get his money back, he still remains an owner of the company and decides its future course of action. That's a very exciting prospect on its own.

Broadening the Landscape of Business

With the entry of social businesses, the marketplace suddenly finds itself with some new and exciting options, and becomes a more interesting, engaging, and competitive place. Social concerns suddenly enter the market place on an equal footing, not through the public relations window.

Social businesses will operate in the same marketplace with PMBs. They will compete with them, try to outmaneuver them, and seek to capture market share from them, just as other businesses do. If a social business is offering a particular product or service that is also available from a PMB, consumers will decide where to buy, just as they now choose among competing PMBs. They will consider price, quality, convenience, availability, brand image, and all the other traditional factors that influence consumer choices today.

Perhaps for some consumers, the social benefits created by the social business will be an additional reason to buy from it—just as some consumers today prefer to patronize companies with a reputation for being worker-friendly, environmentally conscious, or socially responsible. But for the most part, social businesses will compete with PMBs on the same terms as we see in traditional capitalist competition—and may the best company win.

Social businesses will also compete with one another. If two or more social businesses are operating in the same market, consumers will have to decide which one to patronize. Again, product and service quality will probably be the main determining factor for most customers.

In addition, social businesses will compete for potential investors, just as PMBs do. Of course, this will be a different kind of competition than we see among PMBs.

Consider two profit-maximizing businesses that are competing for investment dollars—two auto makers, for example. The competition here will turn on which PMB is perceived as having a greater future profit potential. If most investors believe that company A is likely to be more profitable than company B, they will rush to buy shares of company A stock, because they expect to earn higher dividends in the future, and they also expect to benefit from continuing growth in the overall value (or *equity*) of the company. This launches a positive cycle in which company A stock rises in price, making investors happy.

By contrast, when two social businesses compete for investors, the competition is based not on future profit maximization but on social benefits achieved. Each social business will claim that it is better positioned to serve the people and the planet than its rival, and it will develop and publicize a business plan to support that claim. Would-be social investors will scrutinize those claims carefully. After all, they are planning to invest their money with the goal of benefiting society, and they will want to be sure that their investment does the greatest possible good. Just as a profit-minded investor seeks to maximize expectations of future dividends and equity growth, a social investor wants to find out how close the company is getting in solving the social problem it is addressing.

Thus, competing social businesses will push each other to improve their efficiency and to serve the people and the planet better. This is one of the great powers of the social-business concept: It brings the advantages of free-market competition into the world of social improvement.

Competition in the marketplace of ideas almost always has a powerful positive impact. When a large number of people are vying to do the best possible job of developing and refining an idea—and when the flow of money toward them and their company depends on the outcome of the competition—the overall level of everyone's performance rises dramatically. We see this beneficial effect of competition in many arenas. Intense competition among makers of personal computers, for example, has caused the price of PCs to fall dramatically even as their speed, power, and other features have improved. The rise of Japanese manufacturers of cars and electronic products forced U.S. and European companies to improve the quality of their goods so as to compete for both customers and investors.

By creating a competitive marketplace for social-benefit investing, the concept of social business brings the same kind of positive pressure to bear among those who seek to serve the disadvantaged people of the world.

Competition among social businesses will be different in quality than competition among PMBs. PMB competition is about making more money. If you lose, you get financially hurt. Social business competition will be about pride, about establishing which is the best team to achieve the social objective. Competitors will remain friends. They will learn from each other. They can merge with each other at any time to become a stronger social force. Social businesses are friends dedicated to the same or similar causes. They collaborate to achieve their social goals. They will feel happy to see another social business entering the same area of business, rather than getting worried.

To attract investors, I propose the creation of a separate stock market, which could be called the social stock market. Only social businesses will be listed there. The existence of a public marketplace for trading shares in social businesses will have many benefits. It will create liquidity, making it easy for shareholders to move in and out of social investments, just as they currently do with investments in PMBs. It will generate public scrutiny and evaluation of social businesses, providing a layer of "natural regulation" to supplement any government regulation that will need to be be created to avoid the usual problems of the market place—deception, false reporting, inflated claims, disguised businesses, and so on. And it will raise the public profile of the social-business concept, attracting even more money and energy from investors and entrepreneurs alike.

Two Kinds of Social Businesses

At this stage in the development of the concept of social business, we can only glimpse its general outlines. In the years to come, as social businesses begin to spring up around the world, new features and forms of social business will undoubtedly be developed. But from today's vantage point, I propose two possible kinds of social businesses.

The first I have already described: Companies that focus on providing a social benefit rather than on maximizing profit for the owners, and that are owned by investors who seek social benefits such as poverty reduction, healthcare for the poor, social justice, global sustainability, and so on, seeking psychological, emotional, and spiritual satisfactions rather than financial reward.

The second operates in a rather different fashion: Profit-maximizing businesses that are owned by the poor or disadvantaged. In this case, the social benefit is derived from the fact that the dividends and equity growth produced by the PMB will go to benefit the poor, thereby helping them to reduce their poverty or even escape it altogether.

Notice the differences between these two kinds of social businesses. In the first case, it is the nature of the products, services, or operating systems of the business that creates the social benefit. This kind of social business might provide food, housing, health care, education, or other worthwhile goods to help the poor; it might clean up the environment, reduce social inequities, or work to alleviate ills such as drug and alcohol abuse, domestic violence, unemployment, or crime. Any business that can achieve objectives like these while covering its costs through the sales of goods or services *and* that pays no financial dividend to its investors can be classified as a social business.

With the second type of social business, goods or services produced might or might not create a social benefit. The social benefit created by this kind of company comes from its ownership. Because the ownership of shares of the business belongs to the poor or disadvantaged (as defined by specific, transparent criteria developed and enforced by the company directors), any financial benefit generated by the company's operations will go to help those in need.

Imagine that a poor rural region of a country is separated from the main commercial centers by a river too deep, wide, and wild to be forded by pedestrians or ordinary vehicles. The only way to cross this river is by ferry, which provides expensive, slow, and intermittent service. As a result, the area's poor and low-income residents face economic and social handicaps that depress their incomes, reduce availability of affordable goods, and lower their access to education, health care, and other vital services. In our example, we assume that the national and local governments are unable to address the problem because of lack of funds, political indifference, or other shortcomings. (Although this is a hypothetical example, it accurately describes conditions in much of the developing world.)

Now suppose a private company is formed to build a new highway and a safe, modern bridge to connect the rural area with the commercial center of the country. This company could be structured as a social business in two ways.

First, it could provide access to poor and low-income residents at a discounted toll, while charging a commercial toll to middle- and upper-class residents and to large commercial organizations. (Obviously some kind of means-testing procedure would be needed to verify the eligibility of poor people for the discounted toll; perhaps the same kind of ID card that is used to indicate eligibility for government welfare could be accepted by the toll-takers.) The toll revenues would cover the costs of building, operating, and maintaining the bridge and highway, and, over time, they could be used to repay the funds initially provided by investors. However, those investors would receive no further profits. If profits beyond this are generated by the tolls, they could be used to build additional infrastructure to benefit the rural community—more roads and bridges, for example, or perhaps some social businesses to stimulate the local economy and create jobs.

Second, ownership of the bridge-and-highway company could actually be put in the hands of the poor and lower-income residents of the rural area. This could be done through the sale of low-priced shares, purchased by them with loans provided by microcredit organizations or through credit that is later recouped from the profit of the company. Profits generated by tolls could *either* be invested in new infrastructure projects or paid in the form of dividends to the poor and lower-income residents who own the company, thereby benefiting them in direct financial fashion.

Grameen Bank makes small loans available without collateral and at a reasonable cost to the poor, thereby enabling them to start or expand tiny businesses and ultimately lift themselves out of poverty. Grameen Bank would be a regular PMB if it were owned by well-off investors. But it is not. Grameen Bank is owned by the poor: Ninety-four percent of the ownership shares of the institution are held by the borrowers themselves.

Thus, Grameen Bank is a social business by virtue of its ownership structure. If a big bank like Grameen can be owned by poor women in Bangladesh, any big company can be owned by poor people, if we seriously come up with practical ownership-management models.

And yes, a social business could also combine *both* forms of benefit to the poor: It could follow a business plan designed to produce social benefits through the nature of the goods and services it creates and sells *and also* be owned by the poor or disadvantaged.

Social business is a new idea. But those who have learned about it so far have responded with enthusiasm and excitement. I believe it has the potential to change our world in a fundamental way, liberating the creative energies of millions of people and helping produce solutions to our most serious social problems.

FOR FURTHER

INFORMATION

You may contact Professor Yunus and the Grameen Bank at:

Professor Muhammad Yunus
Grameen Bank
Mirpur Two
Dhaka 1216
Bangladesh
Fax: 8802–8013559
E-mail: *yunus@grameen.net*
Website: *www.grameen.com*

INDEX

Tim Campbell

Muhammad Yunus was born in Chittagong, a seaport in Bangladesh. The third of fourteen children, he was educated at Dhaka University and was awarded a Fulbright scholarship to study economics at Vanderbilt University. He then served as chairman of the economics department at Chittagong University before devoting his life to providing financial and social services to the poorest of the poor. He is the founder and managing director of Grameen Bank and the author of *Creating a World Without Poverty*. Yunus and Grameen Bank are winners of the 2006 Nobel Peace Prize.

PublicAffairs is a publishing house founded in 1997. It is a tribute to the standards, values, and flair of three persons who have served as mentors to countless reporters, writers, editors, and book people of all kinds, including me.

I.F. STONE, proprietor of *I. F. Stone's Weekly*, combined a commitment to the First Amendment with entrepreneurial zeal and reporting skill and became one of the great independent journalists in American history. At the age of eighty, Izzy published *The Trial of Socrates*, which was a national bestseller. He wrote the book after he taught himself ancient Greek.

BENJAMIN C. BRADLEE was for nearly thirty years the charismatic editorial leader of *The Washington Post*. It was Ben who gave the *Post* the range and courage to pursue such historic issues as Watergate. He supported his reporters with a tenacity that made them fearless and it is no accident that so many became authors of influential, best-selling books.

ROBERT L. BERNSTEIN, the chief executive of Random House for more than a quarter century, guided one of the nation's premier publishing houses. Bob was personally responsible for many books of political dissent and argument that challenged tyranny around the globe. He is also the founder and longtime chair of Human Rights Watch, one of the most respected human rights organizations in the world.

• • •

For fifty years, the banner of Public Affairs Press was carried by its owner Morris B. Schnapper, who published Gandhi, Nasser, Toynbee, Truman, and about 1,500 other authors. In 1983, Schnapper was described by *The Washington Post* as "a redoubtable gadfly." His legacy will endure in the books to come.

Peter Osnos, *Founder and Editor-at-Large*